Instant Identity

mediated youth

Sharon Mazzarella
General Editor

Vol. 2

PETER LANG
New York • Washington, D.C./Baltimore • Bern
Frankfurt am Main • Berlin • Brussels • Vienna • Oxford

Shayla Thiel Stern

Instant Identity

Adolescent Girls and the World
of Instant Messaging

PETER LANG
New York • Washington, D.C./Baltimore • Bern
Frankfurt am Main • Berlin • Brussels • Vienna • Oxford

Library of Congress Cataloging-in-Publication Data

Stern, Shayla Thiel.
Instant identity: adolescent girls and the world of instant messaging /
Shayla Thiel Stern.
p. cm. — (Mediated youth; vol. 2)
Includes bibliographical references.
1. Teenage girls—United States—Psychology—Case studies.
2. Instant messaging—Social aspects—United States—Case studies.
3. Teenage girls—Social networks—United States—Case studies.
4. Internet and teenagers—United States—Case studies.
HQ799.2.I5 S84   305.235'20285469—dc22   2006037194
ISBN 978-0-8204-6325-4
ISSN 1555-1814

Bibliographic information published by **Die Deutsche Bibliothek**.
Die Deutsche Bibliothek lists this publication in the "Deutsche
Nationalbibliografie"; detailed bibliographic data is available
on the Internet at http://dnb.ddb.de/.

Cover photograph by Kelli Langdon

The paper in this book meets the guidelines for permanence and durability
of the Committee on Production Guidelines for Book Longevity
of the Council of Library Resources.

© 2007 Peter Lang Publishing, Inc., New York
29 Broadway, 18th floor, New York, NY 10006
www.peterlang.com

Printed in the United States of America

*I dedicate this book to the incredible girls and young women
who assisted in my research and taught me so much about their lives.*

Table of Contents

Acknowledgments

Thank you so much to Sharon Mazzarella, the editor of this book series, who has proved to be not only a brilliant mentor to me but also a great friend. Thanks to all the girls who participated in the research for this book and to their parents who consented to it; I hope that it will be helpful for scholars, parents, educators, and ultimately, thousands of other girls out there. Thank you to Gigi Durham, my graduate adviser who guided me through the research while challenging and encouraging me throughout. I also want to acknowledge members of my graduate school writing group from the University of Iowa: Sarah Burke Odland, Madeleine Shufeldt, Dina Gavrilos, and Julie Ferris; as well as the members of my dissertation committee: Jane B. Singer, Dan Berkowitz, Cynthia Lewis, and Ellen Lewin. I would also like to express my heartfelt thanks to my wonderful friends and family, especially my husband, Matt Stern, for supporting me as I conducted research and wrote the book. Finally, thank you to Damon Zucca, the acquisitions editor from Peter Lang Publishing who originally expressed interest in the book and everyone at Peter Lang who helped with the editing, production, and distribution. And a very special thanks to my former student at DePaul University, Kelli Langdon, for her documentary photo that is on the cover of this book. I believe it perfectly captures IM as a private communication that is a large part of girls' everyday lives.

CHAPTER ONE
Understanding the World of Adolescent Girls and Instant Messaging

Thirteen-year-old Leanne[1] considers herself a typical seventh grader. She doesn't like her social studies teacher but still gets Bs in the class, she enjoys playing basketball and listening to Jesse McCartney, she wears lip gloss but is not allowed to try other makeup yet, and every evening after dinner, she likes to talk to at least ten of her friends on an instantaneous textual communication medium called instant messaging or IM, a technology that is free to anyone who has an Internet account and is able to download it to their computer. If she's lucky, her two sisters (aged fourteen and eleven) and eight-year-old brother will have already taken their turn at using the Internet so that she can converse uninterrupted. If she's really lucky, her mom will be too busy to check in on her and catch what she's writing. Tonight looks to be an especially juicy night for gossip.

For girls like Leanne, IM is more than just a technology. It can be a driving force in their private and public lives, particularly for adolescents who use it. By logging on each night and often carrying on numerous conversations at one time, adolescents hold conversations primarily with people they know and often with people they have already spoken with at school earlier in the day. Through IM, they may hook up and break up, figure out the weekend's math homework, make plans for Friday night, and debrief on the day at school with any number of other friends. Using IM at night helps Leanne and her peers manage a social world that is at once private (as it's navigated alone in bedrooms and dens with just a computer and a keyboard) and very public (because the conversations are so easily transmittable and many may take place at once).

As she types furiously away in the abbreviations and slang that her online friends understand perfectly,[2] it is clear that she is a member of a distinct social network. In fact, she is just one of millions of teens who create and manage their own social worlds through IM. An extensive study conducted by the Pew Research Center on adolescent Internet use says that close to thirteen million teenagers use IM—a number that is growing all the time—and that this technology-driven communication has a key place in many of their lives (Lenhart, Rainie, & Lewis, 2001; Lenhart, Madden, & Hilton, 2005). They use IM to maintain communication with peers throughout their time away from them and also see it as a means of multitasking—another way to maintain constant contact with friends while surfing the Web, writing email, talking on the phone, watching television, and still being in the sightline of their parents (Clark, 2005). It is quickly becoming a preferred mode of communication for teens: 69 percent of those who use IM use it at least several times a week (Lenhart et al., 2001; Lenhart et al., 2005).

Adolescence and Identity: An Introduction to Past Theories
Adolescence is a time when people develop and construct identity and, notably, negotiate feelings of confusion as they straddle childhood and what most would consider some rather "adult" concerns (Erikson, 1950, 1968). This sense of confusion over identity suggests that adolescence is a time of experimentation with different styles of communicating and articulating identity. In light of this, it is notable that 37 percent of adolescent IM users say that they have said something online that they would not have said in person (Lenhart et al., 2001). The implications of online conversation in contributing to adolescents' communication practices and articulation of self in relation to peers have yet to be realized, but the possibility that online communication may be changing these is worthy of study.

Adolescent girls are particularly prone to crises of identity as a result of dominant cultural and media discourses (Brown & Gilligan, 1992; Currie, 1999; Finders, 1996; Mazzarella & Pecora, 1999; McRobbie, 1982, 1997; Milkie, 1999; Orenstein, 1994; Pipher, 1994). They sometimes yearn for an impossible ideal of perfection in the eyes of their parents and peers (Brown & Gilligan, 1992), and they develop both emotional and physical problems, such as eating disorders, as a result (Martin & Gentry, 1997; Pipher, 1994). The media's world of adolescent girls is often characterized as particularly feminized—a world where physical beauty, sexual attractiveness, and product consumption (often that supplants both beauty and sexuality) supercede intelligence and creativity (Currie, 1999; Durham, 1996, 1999; Ferguson, 1983; McRobbie, 1982). These girls yearn for an unattainable perfection and niceness that is at odds with their desire to simply "be themselves," whether that may mean letting physical flaws or less-than-nice behaviors prevail (Brown & Gilligan, 1992; Simmons, 2002). Recent research also shows that the culture of adolescent girls is rife with bullying among girls and that girls are ever prone to cattiness and cliquishness

(Simmons, 2002; Talbot, 2002)—studies that may simplify somewhat the social world of girls, but which foster an increasing need for further study of exclusionary practices among them. This research is important as ever, especially keeping in mind that gender discrimination throughout history placed women and girls at the margins of study and deemed them if not unworthy of serious study, then deviant or emotionally immature (Brown & Gilligan, 1992; Davies, 1993; de Beauvoir, 1949; Gilligan, 1982). This historical inattention to the study of girls' cultural practices has worked to effectively silence girls' voices or lump them together with the voices of boys, not taking into account the important differences produced by gender and the way gender works within culture (Davies, 1993; Orenstein, 1994; Pipher, 1994).

As society moves into the age of the Internet, technology becomes more important in girls' lives as a means to communicate with one another (Lewis & Fabos, 2000; Lewis & Finders, 2002; Thiel, 2005) and articulate their own identities to the world (Chandler, 1998; Stern, 1999, 2001, 2004). Computer-mediated communication also becomes a site of identity play and experimentation (Turkle, 1995). It has been interpreted as both a "safe haven" for open expression and normalized communication among genders (Evard, 1996; Grisso & Weiss, 2005; Stern, 1999; Turkle, 1995) and, conversely, yet another place where voices are often silenced through patriarchal discourses (Durham, 2001; Kendall, 1996).

Keeping in mind this dichotomy between IM as a safe space to experiment with identity and as a space where dominant patriarchal discourses also exist, I wish, in this chapter, to offer an intercession for understanding how adolescent girls, through their uses of IM, negotiate and articulate their identities, especially with regard to gender. Since IM allows for communication without body and actual voice, gender lines can be more easily blurred to allow for an intervention in the negotiation and construction of gender identity. Conversely, it seems that this identity is often played out in ways that are consistent with the real-life construction of "traditional" gender roles. The dichotomy can be understood by examining the conversations held through IM and listening to the voices of girls interviewed about IM's role in their lives.

Explicating Identity

Identity is a complex social construction created and sustained by a subject's location within a culture and a society. Owing to the sharp increase in computer-mediated communication and mediated technologies in general in the past decade or so, it becomes important to examine how identity construction has become increasingly complicated through its articulation in the use of these communication technologies. Disembodiment, like that afforded through online communication, exists in a fast-paced, multinetworked environment across different races, genders, classes, religions, vast geographic locations, provoking myriad questions about how the lack of a body may shape and color one's perception of culture and one's location within culture.

It is at this juncture of cultural perception and cultural location that the concept of identity demands new attention. Ultimately there is no one absolute identity because identity is bound up in cultural discourse or dominant notions of what it is to exist and behave in the context of society and culture (Foucault, 1974). From the moment of birth, humans mark themselves (and are marked by others) as they exist within cultural ideologies (such as family, educational system, politics and government, religion, etc.). They cannot exist outside of the ideological systems—and discourses—that surround them because within these systems, humans believe they are in charge of how they behave, identify themselves, and function (Althusser, 1968/1970). However, this is an illusion based on a person's understanding of the system; humans are born as subjects of these belief systems and are thus interpellated (or "hailed") by the ideology constantly surrounding them (Althusser, 1968/1970, p. 245).

Judith Butler (1990) takes up the idea of hailing in her assertion that gender identity is a performed construction based upon dominant cultural discourses. Females and males "perform" what they interpret their gender to be based upon, what their culture has taught them is the correct (heterosexual) interpretation of gender; for instance, that girls are "nice" and wear pink and boys are "boisterous" and wear blue. Stuart Hall (1996) furthers our understanding of the ever-shifting nature of identity, pronouncing it "never unified or coherent," except when people wish to "construct a comforting story," or what Hall calls a "narrative of the self" as a way to feel some coherence about who they are and how they exist within culture (Hall, 1996, p. 277). Identity constantly shifts throughout a person's life and throughout daily experiences and, as Hall (1996) has argued, is in fact, fragmented, which hearkens back to Althusser's idea that fragmentation is a product of the subject being hailed by the ideological systems within which she exists.

In the disembodied world of the Internet, identity is complicated through the notion of representation. Although many studies have discussed online representation in terms of falsehoods based on people intentionally misleading one another (regarding their race, gender, class, and other markers of identity), others have discussed identity in terms of "play" and experimentation through behavior, as well as conversational, and textual manipulation (Stephenson, 1988; Turkle, 1995). Prevalent in nearly all research published on the topic is the representation of gender through online communication.

The study of identity within a computer-mediated environment offers a unique means to facilitate and grasp the fluidity of gender. In a 1993 issue of the *New Yorker*, an often-cited cartoon shows two dogs sitting at a computer, with one dog saying to the other: "No one knows if you're a dog in cyberspace." Indeed, no one knows whether persons are male, female, or a combination of both, unless they choose to signal gender to them through discourse—and even then, this may be an elaborate performance of gender or a play with identity that has little to do with the body a person owns in real life.

Theories about gender identity also generate claims about social roles and preferences that shift within this new environment. By understanding the process of identity construction, we may also understand the degree to which such roles and preferences are conveyed online. Central to this particular study is the notion that social roles and preferences are formed in large part before adulthood—specifically, during adolescence (Erikson, 1950; Lesko, 2001). Much of media and technology usage is tangled up with adolescents' notions of the "real world." This age group is often acculturated into a patriarchal system of meaning making, which is in large part an effect of the dominant mediated discourses surrounding them in conversations with parents and teachers (Finders, 1996), fashion magazines (Currie, 1999; Duke, 2000; Duke & Kreshel, 1998; Durham, 1996; McRobbie, 1982, 1997; Milkie, 1994), romance novels (Christian-Smith, 1993; Rogers-Cherland, 1994), and the Internet and other computer-mediated technologies (Currie, 1999; Durham, 2001; Lewis & Finders, 2002; Sefton-Green, 1998; Stern, 1999; Thiel, 2005; Walsh, 2005). In romance fiction, women readers are provided "vicarious emotional nurturance" through identification with a fictional heroine whose identity as a woman is confirmed primarily by the sexual and romantic attentions of an idealized male hero (Radway, 1984, p. 112). Adolescent romance novels offer cultural stereotypes of what constitutes young womanhood and constructions of femininity shaped by configurations of power and control (Christian-Smith, 1993; Rogers-Cherland, 1994).

Although some adolescents resist these mediated discourses, the discourse of resistance is not the one that is most often articulated in schools or the media (Davies, 1993; Mazzarella, 1999). In other words, there are few discursive alternatives available that demonstrate differentially gendered positions in the world of adolescents. For example, boys are often steered toward careers and "logical" sciences whereas girls are steered toward consumerism and romance. This defies the current career patterns of women internationally as more and more women use their skills to pursue technologically focused careers (Thiel, 2004; Walker, 2001). Worse, it may perpetuate a notion among adolescent girls that they are constructed and validated through the (heterosexual) eyes of the opposite sex (Willinsky & Hunniford, 1993), and often drowns a resistant discourse. The result may be a culture of adolescence that is often confusing for girls who may seek alternative discourses from which to construct alternative identities or who wish to construct a comfortable identity while still attempting to fit in with peers and attain a media-perfect version of reality (Mazzarella & Pecora, 1999; Orenstein, 1994; Pipher, 1994). Some research demonstrates this opportunity to construct alternative identities—or even to become comfortable with the identities they have currently appropriated—through online communication (Clark, 2005; Sefton-Green, 1998; Turkle, 1995). Mediated communication provides a vast landscape upon which we can better understand adolescents' identity negotiations, but there is a particular need for study on the cultural narratives that manifest themselves through interactive media.

Identity and Gender: Exploring Social Roles as Construct and Performance

Gender, like identity, is definable on many parameters. Going back more than a half century, Simone de Beauvoir, in speaking of the identity of woman, focused on the enculturation process involved in "becoming" woman. She notes that women were not born, but rather they constructed themselves to become the gender of woman, or at least "woman" as the role was understood through the patriarchal cultural discourses of the time (de Beauvoir, 1949). In a more detailed explanation of what this means, Butler (1990) explains that women are not born enacting a gender that is inherently feminine, but they learn to act like women by performing a culturally learned version of womanhood in a stylized repetition of acts from girlhood to adulthood.

Subjects construct and affirm identity through far more than the underlying meaning-making process about gender. In fact, it is thought by some to be impossible to discuss identity in only these terms. Identity should be considered through the lenses of gender, age, race, class, geographical location—really, any *particular* situation that in any way marks a person in a *particular* way—in order to be best understood in all its shifting intricacies (Abu-Lughod, 1990). All actions and texts are constituted around a particular discourse—or even multiple discourses—and readers make sense of them in relation to the discourses [of age, race, gender, class, region, and so on] through which their consciousness makes sense of social reality (Foucault, 1974; Longhurst, 1989). Therefore, though gender is paramount to this study of IM, these other factors are as important to this project and any study of identity.

The Internet as a Site for Identity Play

Since the inception of the Internet and the explosion of computer-mediated communication, scholars from various fields have sought to explore the sociological and cultural underpinnings of online identity formation. Much of the work has taken a cultural studies approach to investigate communication and culture within virtual communities and digital culture. The bulk of this work offers the theory that online conversations lead to the formation of distinct online identities that might be the same or entirely different from a person's "real-world" identity, which is based in part on psychological theory that assumes the existence of a "real" or core identity (Bromberg, 1996; Reid, 1991; Rheingold, 1993; Turkle, 1995). However, this work is at odds with the poststructuralist notion that there is no "real" core identity, but rather many identities constantly shifting, depending on the cultural discourse being appropriated or negotiated at a given time; it should be noted that although psychologists—and much of the population outside academe— agree with the notion of a core identity, this chapter takes up the poststructuralist view that identity is not fixed. More useful in this theoretical framework is Turkle's concept of "windowing," a widely cited metaphor designed to describe a person who "distributes" himself or herself into multiple online conversations and acts differently among the conversations, taking on different roles all at the same time (Turkle, 1995). This is a common practice among IM users (Lewis & Fabos, 2000; Thiel, 2005) and can seem very empowering. It posits that when online, limitations of real-world bodies may be overcome as well, as its participants "by-pass the boundaries delineated by cultural constructs of beauty, ugliness, and fashion" (Reid, 1991, p. 42) and overcome the boundaries of gender, race, class, and age (Haraway, 1991; Reid, 1991).

When viewed as a process of constant negotiation, identity construction can also be seen as playful or empowering, especially as it takes place within online communication. Dery (1994) proposes that the disembodied nature of online communication frees users from the threat of reprimand resulting from normative behavioral lapses. Moreover, the scholars who have studied online communities refer to a "transcendence" that often takes place among persons who hope to use online identity to grasp at higher social standing or even a realization of dreams (Bromberg, 1996; Lewis & Fabos, 2000; Turkle, 1995).

In order to transcend, however, participants of computer-mediated communication first tend to explore *alternate* identities. Although this means taking on an entirely different role or persona within a conversation, research has demonstrated that users just as often seek to maintain an identity consistent with their real-world identity (Irain Bowker, 2001; Lewis & Finders, 2002). Most often in instant-relay chat or IM, users adhere to a consistent presentation of themselves to acquaintances although they might experiment with different tones, voices, and subject content among the different persons with whom they communicate (Lewis & Fabos, 2000; Reid, 1991; Thiel, 2005). And often, frequent Internet users are presented with the same dominant gendered discourses online they encounter in offline media on a daily basis (Sefton-Green, 1998). Online identity construction and manipulation appears to be an enormous consideration in this communication process among adolescents. Negotiation is often located directly through the discourse of online communication—specifically through language use, social networking, and power negotiation among peers, as well as a general surveillance of the social online landscape (Lewis & Fabos, 2000; Sefton-Green, 1998). However, scholars have found that rather than actually pretending to be someone else, the only place where some adolescents may feel comfortable expressing what they feel to be their "true" identity is in fact online (Tobin, 1998, p. 123), and they acknowledge a pureness (Clark, 1998) in their online relationships that is not present in their real-world ones.

Online gender identity negotiation might present a new opportunity for girls who might have felt silenced within their home and school culture because it allows for communication and identity articulation without the worry that can go along with face-to-face contact. Girls use the technology of the Internet not only to engage in two-way (or many-way) communication with their peers but they also use it to construct Web pages (Stern, 1999, 2001), to constantly update blogs and live journals (Bortree, 2005; Fillion, 2005; Kornblum, 2005), to create pages on social networking sites like MySpace (Dahl, 2006; Kornblum, 2006), and, more recently, to broadcast their own podcasts (Ishizuka, 2006)—all ways of using new media technologies and in the process, evoking a self-perception of identity and sharing with anyone who will read or listen. Although the notion that girls are natural innovators and consumers of technology seems to oppose the dominant notion that links masculinity more strongly with technology and technofetishism, technology is often thought to empower the less powerful, making physical strength and presence less necessary in many ways—and making the Internet a particularly good avenue for feminine articulation of identity (Haraway, 1991). Furthermore, although girls are often viewed as passive consumers of media by the corporate mainstream media that attempts to sell them on a particular type of adolescence based on romanticism, consumerism, fashion, beauty, celebrities, and elements of "romantic individualism" (McRobbie, 1997), the Internet allows them to turn the tables on the corporate mainstream media and demonstrate that they are in fact able to produce culture themselves through their conversations and postings (Mazzarella, 2005). In recent years, scholars have begun to acknowledge that girls have emerged as cultural producers who create cultural artifacts—Web pages, blogs, and IM conversations, for example—and that this emergence is one of the most important occurrences within youth culture in the past twenty years (Kearney, 1998).

Although IM is very much a conversational medium, the idea that there is an audience for the text becomes paramount when trying to understand how identity is enacted when adolescents use it to communicate with one another. Stuart Hall (1981) first explained the encoding/decoding model of the relationship between text and audience: the text is encoded by the producer and decoded by the reader, and there may be major differences between two different readings of the same code. However, by using recognized codes and conventions, and by relying upon audience expectations, the producers can position the audience and thus create a certain amount of agreement on what the code means. This is known as preferred reading. In IM, this notion is challenged to a certain extent: The conversants sometimes appear to be talking in what indeed is a secret, teenage code rife with abbreviations and slang, but in the typing, each knows that his or her audience will understand exactly what he or she is talking about.[3] (And when writing for an adult audience, the teens generally do not use the same conventions but instead appropriate what they perceive to be a more "adult" form of writing.) Because of this, the producer of the text no longer holds the privileged position of controlling the message; the power is divided equally between producer and audience because they are one and the same. The extremely high level of interactivity not only differentiates it from the mediated communications to which Hall referred, but IM is also quite different from other interpersonal and mass communication methods and technologies and is worthy of study in its own right. Its real-time nature distinguishes it from email, which can be edited and reformatted endlessly in the same way that an old-fashioned letter or telegram might be. Its privileging of written text (text that can quickly and easily be copied and sent to different recipients) over oral conversation differentiates it from the telephone. IM conversations can be viewed as both a real-time exchange of information and ideas among a number of people but yet saved and printed out for future viewing; they represent a particular blurring of private conversation and public space, and because of this, they represent an exceptionally interesting landscape upon which real-world identities may be socially constructed in a virtual context.

Above: *AOL's Instant Messenger or AIM allows users to type their end of the conversation in the lower box while the entire conversation with the reply from their "buddy" appears in the upper box. Most of the girls who participated in this study used AIM.*

In this book, I attempt to understand how this intriguing, unique new medium might provide a site in which we can further understand identity construction among adolescent girls—the population that appears to rely most heavily upon it for daily communication (Lenhart & Madden, 2005; Lenhart, Madden & Hilton, 2005; Lenhart et al. 2001). In doing so, I propose to answer two questions: What are the cultural narratives and representations used by girls in IM? How does this online practice contribute to the construction of gender identity in adolescent girls? In this analysis, I will locate IM and its many functions and roles within our culture—including its power to sell to a coveted demographic—and better understand how girls are at once powerful cultural producers within this new media and yet, still consumers who may buy into the corporate messages meant to pigeonhole them within media stereotypes associated with teen girls since the early part of the twentieth century. The following section further examines the various corporate influences within IM.

Corporate Influences on Instant Messaging

This apparent freedom from the traditional producer–consumer model of communication and from the limitations of noninteractive text may be constrained by the technological process itself. Although the IM technologies are free to any person using the Internet, they are deployed by America Online (or AOL, which is owned by Time Warner) and Microsoft (through the Microsoft Network or MSN), two of the largest media conglomerates in the world. In order to understand how the narratives of IM are shaped, we must understand the cultural context of these discourses. Paramount to understanding the context for these discourses is grasping the conditions of production that go into controlling the deployment of the technology. In this case, it is important to understand the history and corporate production modes associated with the Internet, the medium that in numerous ways controls the message and provides a landscape containing dominant discourses that often marginalize women and girls.

The Internet was once known as a realm burgeoning with community discussions that were free from dominant cultural and commercial discourses (Rheingold, 1993; Turkle, 1995), but as more people logged on over the past decade or so, corporations saw an opportunity to attract more business.

Today, their messages and the prevalent cultural discourses within them permeate the once-commercial-free Internet. Girls in past media studies have been positioned as heavy consumers—a notion normalized in such mass media as teen magazines (Currie, 1999; McRobbie 1982)—and IM could be yet another avenue of consumption. Although it would seem that corporatization would be an unlikely part of actual online conversations between users such as those held on IM, it might slowly be making inroads there, too. This already has been demonstrated in conversations by some of the adolescent girls who participated in the research for this book as they invoke product names and yearn for certain ideals of physical attractiveness that are often espoused by the companies selling these products.

One means of packaging and advertising is through the AIM Today page, a page that launches automatically when users log in to AOL's Internet version of IM (this feature may be turned off at the time of registration for IM). Another method of advertising is through what AIM calls "buddy icons." The "AIM Today" page often features a headline urging users to "Download Buddy Icons," referring to small icons that may appear in the window where the IM conversation is taking place. It is free to download the icons, and some of them are generic clip art iconography and photos (e.g., an icon representing a zodiac sign or a happy face) whereas the majority is actual product advertisements. Free icons may be changed as often as the user likes; other "premium" icons are available at a price of $9.95 per year or $1.95 per month. More savvy users can learn how to download their own picture or favorite photo or advertisement to use as an icon. Although adolescents may say that they do not pay any attention to the advertising and marketing efforts of companies like AOL and MSN, the messages sent out by such companies are still viewed by the users who just glance at them on a daily basis. Often the intent behind such content is to encourage them not only to read the content and buy the products advertised but also to buy into the particular lifestyles represented within the content (Currie, 1999; McRobbie, 1982). Chapter Five provides further analysis into how the corporate entities behind IM target girls as consumers and whether girls are buying.

What, Why, and How? Background and Methodology

Keeping in mind the many ways that adolescent girls may use IM to negotiate and construct gender identity, this book explores a number of topics related to the world of IM that may be of interest not only to scholars who study teens and online communication, but also to parents and teachers who have tried to understand what teens are up to when they hammer away at their keyboards both at home and school. The research included in this book focuses on a dozen different girls of different racial and class backgrounds located in different parts of the country and analyzes the IM conversations they hold with a variety of classmates and friends. Although the girls are quite different from one another, each agreed that IM was a very important means of controlling their social world and articulating their views, wants, and needs to peers. Within this social world, there are common concerns that are of utmost importance in the hearts of teens, such as popularity and social standing and how both play out within IM, and there are facets of IM that adolescents most likely do not even consider—such as its capacity to act as a diary or a space for rebellion.

Investigating the use of IM is complicated because the act of IM is usually solitary and in private, relegated primarily to adolescents' homes and during nonschool hours. Often, they are online for hours carrying on these conversations; when printed, these conversations sometimes generate more than twenty pages per evening. IM, which is practiced most often in complete privacy, creates a subcultural space in which the identity process is enacted among adolescent girls. In an attempt to gain entrée to this subcultural space and better understand their thought process and creation of meaning through virtual conversation, I used a combination of in-depth and ongoing interviews with the girls. All girls, however, were avid users of IM who spent between ten and thirty hours a week on their home computers. In addition to having girls email me IM conversations (between eight and forty per girl over a period of several months) and doing in-depth interviews, I conducted ongoing IM conversations with a number of girls to clarify and contextualize some of the conversations they sent me. In addition, I returned to ask a couple of the girls questions years after they initially sent me IM conversations and discussed how its role in their lives has changed or stayed the same. Although their parents were not officially part of the study, I did speak to some of them in the process of gaining permission for their daughters to participate in the study, and in those conversations, I often gained valuable insights on parental interpretations of their children's behavior.

Furthermore, my methodology draws from the philosophy of feminist ethnography, a genre that calls for a combination of methods and acknowledgment of power structures within culture in order to create a "feminist ethnography landscape" (Bell, 1993, p. 29). Feminist ethnography also takes into consideration the hegemonic nature of anthropology as a discipline rooted in the idea that a "researcher" studies and reports on (an often exotic) "subject," and attempts to dismantle this relationship by placing the studied subject on a more equal footing as the researcher (Behar & Gordon, 1995; Visweswaran, 1994). Most importantly, I will focus on the *cultural narratives* that manifest themselves through both the girls' conversations and their interviews. These narratives are integral to identity construction (Davies, 1993; Foucault, 1974; Gee, 1999). Through narratives, persons give meaning to their lives and construct themselves; narratives are crucial to shaping personal and social identity and to understanding and constructing the identities of others, and this often plays out in very gendered ways (McLaren, 1993). Walker (2001) says that all narratives are constructed discursively through the common "gender scripts" so that identities and processes of identification occur within the social networks and power relations that are most familiar in society (Walker, 2001). Munro (1998) claims that studying narratives might "highlight gendered constructions of power, resistance and agency" (p. 7)—particularly shedding light upon the social relations that create and maintain gendered norms and power structures. Moreover, narratives have proven effective in gender communication research in large part because women's (and men's, for that matter) stories are often filled with latent meanings (Clair, 1993; Taylor & Conrad, 1992). Narratives are a crucial part of the identity process among children and adolescents. As Davies (1993, p. 17) writes in *Shards of glass: Children reading & writing beyond gendered discourse,* "Each child must locate and take up as their own, narratives of themselves that knit together the details of their existence." She goes on to point out that children must also "learn to be coherent members of others' narratives. Through stories (they) each constitute (themselves) and each other as beings with specificity" (Davies, 1993, p. 17).

Upon reviewing the girls' IM conversations and interview data, I was able to discern a number of themes from the cultural narratives that occurred in each girl's conversations and interviews. I searched for themes, language, and signals that indicated what Gee calls "situated identity," or ways of "performing and recognizing characteristic identities and activities; and ways of coordinating and getting coordinated by other people, things, tools, technologies, symbol systems, places, and times" (Gee, 1999, p. 38). Gee suggests asking a number of questions to help identify narratives and themes such as "What cultural models are relevant here? What must I assume people feel, value, and believe consciously or not, in order to talk (write), act, and/or interact this?" (Gee, 1999, p. 78). "Are there differences here between the cultural models that are affecting espoused beliefs and those that are affecting actions and practices?" (Gee, 1999, p. 79).

Again, it should be emphasized that conversational analysis is an interpretive process, further complicated in this dissertation study by the fact that IM conversations tend to ramble for pages at a time, often with seemingly banal subject matter and slang understood only by the persons using it. To a person who has never used or encountered IM, the pages and pages of conversation resemble a screenplay or script in which each person communicating is represented by a "log-in name" (below, this is the name to the left of the colon) followed by their conversation. Often, the log-in names are chosen to be playful designations for those conversing, and the language used is generally in short, choppy sentences often employing acronyms and slang. The following is an example:

runnergrrl: so whats goin on with u and sam?
TT84: i dunno

In order to maintain validity throughout my study, I attempted to make as few assumptions as possible while conducting the fieldwork and instead waited to analyze all of the conversations and interviews at the end of the data-gathering process. Moreover, at Lindlof's suggestion that the researcher first examine and then acknowledge and overcome her prejudices, I have tried to recognize my own prejudices and personal understanding of cultures, but like Lindlof, I realize this is probably an "endless task" (Lindlof, 1995, p. 216). I do believe the combination of IM conversations and the interviews—both in-depth from the start and throughout the fieldwork process—provides some necessary triangulation that helps to maintain validity.

Who? Meet the Participants

I originally recruited fourteen girls for the study through word-of-mouth requests, though only twelve actually participated in the study. Most of them were friends and acquaintances of my friends and relatives, and in a few cases, the girls recruited their own friends to assist as well, creating a snowball effect that is common within ethnographic studies. Because the early part of adolescence is such a crucial time in the construction of identity and because this age group tends to use IM at a particularly high rate, the girls were all in seventh, eighth, and ninth grades, between the ages of twelve and fifteen. Furthermore, they were recruited under the guidelines of the University of Iowa's Institutional Review Board (IRB) and Office on Human Subjects, and they were required to sign consent forms themselves and receive parental permission to participate. They were also required to tell the persons with whom they conversed over IM that the conversation might be sent to a researcher to study and that all identifying characteristics (log-in names, given names, etc.) would be erased from the final product. I should note that this particular requirement was entirely up to girls participating and it is difficult to say whether they disclosed the research to those they conversed with; these conversational partners were not required to get parental permission, though it could be argued that they are even more anonymous without doing permission slips because I never knew any of their real names or anything specific about them at all. Although I spent a total of eight months collecting data, they sent me conversations at their own discretion over a four-to-six-month range of time, depending on when they were recruited for the study. I received between five and eighteen conversations from each girl over this period of time, although each said that she had many, many more than what she chose to send. My pilot study was done in the late part of 2001 and early part of 2002 whereas the later bulk of the research was done in early spring through the summer of 2003.

The primary group of girls who participated in my research included ten white girls, two African American girls, one Korean American girl, and one Korean girl who spent the previous three years in the United States with her family but had returned to Korea a few months before I interviewed her. The group comprised of mostly Christians (predominantly Catholics), with one Jewish, and another whose family celebrated elements of Buddhism and Christianity. The others did not identify with a particular religion. Their geographic locations ranged from communities with populations of around five thousand to cities with well over a million, and all but one lived in the United States. The notion of social class is important to this book's research because of issues associated with digital divide or access to computer technologies that is strongly divided within society by economic factors and social class. Social class is a constructed category due to its ambiguous relationship to income, occupational status, taste, and lifestyle (Swartz, 1997), and because I was not able to gather accurate information on their parents' income levels, I was not able to label the girls within certain social classes. Moreover, because they are from varied geographical locations, income would have to be taken in the context of cost of living. Instead, I shall simply describe the girls and their families, using my own observations and their interview narratives, and employ what anthropologist Geertz called "thick description" (1973) to give readers a better understanding of their lives. Since each of the girls had a computer and an Internet connection in their homes, it can be inferred that each of them belonged to a family with steady and sufficient income to afford these amenities, which means they most likely would be considered to be above the status of lower middle class. In the descriptions, I use my observations and interview notes to describe the girls' personal styles, attitudes, interests, frustrations, likes, and dislikes; these descriptions not only describe the girls' lives and cultures but also explain how very different the girls are from one another—and they imply a diversity among the study participants that is another marker of validity. In the interest of maintaining privacy and ensuring confidentiality, all of the girls' real names and computer log-in names (as well as all the names of persons mentioned in their IM conversations and their friends' log-in names) are fictitious. I chose the names based on mnemonic devices that would help me remember who each of the girls were, and I attempted to match the names somewhat to contemporary popular names or names that were somewhat popular within the girls' given ethnic groups. Although I do not include conversations from all of the girls in this book, I did examine all of them and used much of their interview data to supplement my conclusions.

In March 2003, I met Jordan, a thirteen-year-old, who lived in an affluent section of southeast Chicago and attended a public magnet school catering specifically to seventh through twelfth graders with a high aptitude for math and science. Jordan's parents—who I knew through a consulting work that I was doing at the time—owned a successful family business that operated in downtown Chicago. They were both extremely proud of Jordan's many accomplishments, particularly her newly acquired computer programming skills, and were eager to talk about her. After I explained my study to them, they volunteered her for the study, saying she would "get a kick" out of helping me and suggested that I email her about it. I promptly scheduled an interview with her at their business office. Jordan's mastery of adult conversational skill belied her adolescent appearance: short brown hair, braces on her teeth, standard T-shirt and jeans from Old Navy. Articulate and soft-spoken, Jordan said that she was not one of the "popular" kids at school but that she had a core group of both male and female friends, and that she really enjoyed playing computer games (NeoPets and Sims—two interactive games—were her favorites) and programming. She showed me a short, rather funny program that she and a friend had done as a class project that was the equivalent of an interactive fill-in-the-blank game, and she spoke of the nuisance of having to attend Hebrew school in preparation for her bat mitzvah, which would take place later in the year.

Through Jordan I met her friend Eunsong, who was also thirteen and lived in Seoul, Korea, but who had spent the previous three years in Chicago attending the same public magnet school. Before returning to Korea several months before, she lived in the United States with her mother while her father worked as a visiting professor at one of the local universities. I interviewed her by email only, where she wrote that she had moved back to Korea at the start of the school year in 2003, and she said that she often found herself missing her friends from Chicago, especially Jordan. She used IM as her primary mode of communication with her American friends (though she said she used her cellphone's text messaging function far more often with her Korean friends—a newer mode of instant communication that is not explored in this book). In her email interview, Eunsong said she hoped that IM and email would help her retain a good command of the English language but that already, only six months after leaving the United States, she was forgetting sentence structure and slang terminology and feeling a little alienated from her former peers because of it. She said that the language and slang terms on IM changed so quickly that it became confusing.

Beth and Leanne, two white sisters from a rural Midwestern community of five thousand, were next to sign on to the project. Beth, at age fourteen, was experiencing a tough adolescence as her father had suddenly died only a couple years before and relations with her mother had become strained in the aftermath. Beth herself had recently sprouted up six inches, making her taller than most of her classmates, and recently had been fitted for glasses (she admitted she would like to get contacts as soon as possible). Often quiet and lethargic in her interviews with me, Beth said that she took refuge in school-sponsored basketball, volleyball, track, and dance lessons, but that she was often required to babysit her younger siblings when her mother went to work during the day. The other siblings (ages seven, nine, twelve, and fourteen) constantly battled each other for computer time. In the course of the study, Beth IMed me frequently just to chat and once confided that she was being ignored by most of her usual IM buddies because of a fight at school; she said I was her only IM partner for the few weeks that the IM exclusion took place.

Her sister, Leanne, twelve and a half, was pretty and quite popular, and though she was also soft-spoken, her quick, dry wit won her friends and kept her on the computer for more hours than Beth IMing her girlfriends. Her grades had been suffering over the past year, which her school psychologist said it might be a result of attention deficit disorder. After she was treated for it, she seemed to be improving in her classes and succeeding in after-school sports. The girls each struggled with the isolation of living on a farm about five miles from the town where they attended a small Catholic school and where all their friends lived; even at twelve and fourteen, both expressed the desire to start driving cars as soon as possible with the hope of "getting off the farm." Their mother, who spent long hours working at a career in real estate, often sped home from work to take the children to their evening activities, and all of them tended to stay up rather late, catching up, making sure homework was finished, and "playing" on the computer.

I met Cara (also white), fourteen, through Beth and Leanne, who were her cousins but were not close: they socialized with her only at family gatherings on holidays even though she lived just thirty minutes from them in slightly larger community. The daughter of a nurse and photographer who attended eighth grade at her community's public middle school, Cara was constantly characterized as a tomboy by the people around her, though she described herself as "sporty." Although she had a positive and playful attitude, Cara tended to get in trouble at school for talking in class, and had lots of male friends. Her one close female friend, Ashley, was another cousin who was two grades behind her in school. Although the same age as Beth, Cara was very different from Beth. Whereas Cara dressed in messy pajama bottoms and layered T-shirts, often wearing a stocking cap even indoors, Beth wore the latest fashions from Gap, carried a purse, and wore her long dark hair neatly pulled out of her face. Cara's mother reported that as a small child, one of Cara's favorite accomplishments was to urinate while standing, "like a boy." Because the family's computer needed repair early into the study, Cara only interviewed with me and sent a few IM conversations; in phone interviews with her after the computer died, she expressed indifference over no longer being able to use IM (something most other girls in the study said would "devastate" their social lives). She said that she felt comfortable saying whatever she wanted in person.

Introduced by a friend, Emma was a white, fifteen-year-old from Baton Rouge, Louisiana, whose parents had recently divorced and delved into a nasty custody battle over her that resulted in her spending half the week with her mother and half the week with her father, who had moved down the street. Although she did not want to discuss her feelings about her parents in her email interview with me, she did say that she felt her life had not changed all that much as a result of the divorce except for the inconvenience of living in two different places. Her older sister had graduated from high school the previous year and was attending college out of state, and Emma said that she missed her but the two still spoke on the phone and sent IMs to each other frequently. Emma acknowledged that she never liked the large public high school that she attended but loved to go there to socialize with her friends (her cousin, my friend, had told me she was very popular in school). A self-described "wild" teenager, Emma estimated that she spent about three hours per night on the computer, most of the time IMing her friends with the latest gossip.

A former colleague from Washington, DC, introduced me (via email) to an African-American fifteen-year-old named Nicole, who lived in a Maryland suburb of DC that is known for its working-class, mostly, African-American population. She had moved there from New Jersey the previous year with her mom and stepfather, who both worked in different mid-level capacities for the county government (she was not sure of their titles or what they did, but she thought each "supervised some people" and "weren't bosses"). Although Nicole's friends in her previous school never used IM, she learned quickly that it was a major part of the social life in her new Maryland public high school and insisted that her parents get an Internet connection as soon as possible. They obliged though they monitored her time on the computer very strictly when they were home. (She said that in an effort to gain more socializing time, she spent the bulk of her time on IM just after she got home from school before her parents arrived from work and before her eighteen-year-old sister made it home from her after-school activities.) She felt that IM made her transition into a new school easier than it might have been if she'd been forced to make friends the old-fashioned way—in person. Passionate about hip-hop and pop music and planning to audition for the school's step team,[3] the outgoing Nicole said in her phone interview that she would love to one day work in the music industry in a business capacity.

Nicole introduced me to her new best friend, Aza, also African-American and recently fifteen, who also spent as many hours as possible on IM in the evening but whose parents also watched her closely and kept the computer in the living room where this made the task a little easier. Aza's mother was a hairstylist and her father worked for a grocery store chain. Though both Aza and Nicole conversed a lot with one another on IM, they also talked with lots of other friends. Although the bulk of these friends were also African Americans, a good number were white or "something else," Nicole said. She said that she really did not consider the other person's race when she was speaking to them online. She said that she always "talked the same way to everyone." Indeed, her conversational voice in IM employed a great deal of "black slang"—drawing from hip-hop culture and elsewhere, and she used this style of speaking with every person with whom she conversed though her tone tended to change depending on the person's gender and age as well as how close she was to the particular person. In her final email to me that accompanied the last round of IM conversation attachments, she discarded her usual slang and wrote, "I have a lot of drama in my life that i hope i can overcome within the rest of the year. So just let me know what you think. Thank you!"

Sunny was a fifteen-year-old whose family immigrated to a Midwestern college town from Korea five years ago and who considered IM to be one of the more important tools for maintaining her social life. Because there were three computers with Internet connections in her home, Sunny said that spending time on the computer was not a problem but that her mother sometimes monitored her usage and that caused her to use guarded language in her IM conversations. Although her mother was home most of the time, at the time of this study, her father worked as a college professor in Korea—a temporary situation, she said. Somewhat quiet in person and very serious about excelling at her public high school (although Sunny said that she and her seventeen-year-old sister consistently received As, her parents hired graduate students from the university to tutor them, and I met Sunny through one of these tutors), she often dressed somewhat provocatively—though fashionably—and wore more makeup than one usually sees on typical

Midwestern teens. When asked about her fashion preferences, she said that she liked to express herself and that her mom said that her clothing choices were fine as long as she did not expose her navel or wear tops that were too low cut; she said she also loved to shop and wear designer clothing. She said that she no longer felt such a strong attachment to her Korean identity and spoke exclusively English (except with her parents), and that she had friends of all kinds of racial and cultural backgrounds now, though she did enjoy spending time with her older sister. However, her conversations with peers demonstrate a range of identity exploration and negotiation in terms of race, class, and religion that tend to betray her insistence on her Americanized, homogenous existence.

Lindsay, almost fifteen-years-old and white was introduced by a relative of mine and lived on a farm approximately ten miles from the town where she attended school. Her mom was a teacher and her dad a construction worker and farmer. Lindsay was the kind of adolescent who participated in every possible activity offered by her school—band, chorus, drama, volleyball, track, basketball, student council, Students Against Drunk Driving, Future Farmers of America—and excelled at every one. Popular, tall, and thin, Lindsay also seemed to be mature and very strong emotionally. Her mother, a teacher, had battled cancer recently and was currently in remission, and her father farmed and recently had taken a second job driving a truck to supplement their income; despite the stress she acknowledged had faced her and her family, Lindsay maintained a positive attitude about her. She had transferred to a new high school two years before in part because the students there tended to get accepted at better colleges, and the female athletes in particular won good athletic scholarships (and she admitted the switch was partly because she wanted something new and different). She was already being courted by a number of colleges in her sophomore year for both track and volleyball scholarships. Although she was poised in person, she said that she also considered IM a very important means of communication for her because it allowed her to "say what she really thinks" without feeling shy or embarrassed. (Lindsay participated in a pilot study for this book's research at the age of fourteen, and I have continued to speak with her about IM and its place in her life. She is now a nineteen-year-old college freshman, and she updated her feelings about IM in recent years.)

Three girls from the grade behind Lindsay (but on the same basketball team and somewhat friendly with Lindsay) agreed to participate in the study as well. They agreed to interview with me together over some pizza. Whitney, whose father was a school administrator and whose mother was a teacher in another district, was a stunningly pretty, articulate fifteen-year-old who said she spent an hour or two each night using IM. Maggie, whose father was an engineer at a factory in a nearby city and whose mother stayed at home with her and her siblings, was an athletic almost fifteen year old who recently had her braces removed and had a serious boyfriend whom she had dated for seven months. Her classmate and next-door neighbor, Caitlyn, looked much older than her fifteen years but giggled and joked comfortably about school and her social life like a typical girl her age. Caitlyn's mother was a nurse and her father a mid-level manager at a company in a nearby city; she said her home life was somewhat atypical because her brother and sister were each five and nine years older than her, making her feel like an only child. Although the girls—who characterized themselves as best friends who all shared not only a passion for basketball and softball but also their feeling of "total boredom" in the town in which they lived—said they generally spoke to one another over the phone they all communicated with classmates and other friends almost exclusively by IM.

Other girls participated in the study to a lesser extent than these, but because I am using some of the information from their interviews, I think it is important to acknowledge them. Anne, a fourteen-year-old daughter of a Methodist minister and stay-at-home mom in rural Iowa, said that even though all of her classmates spent hours online chatting with one another after school and even though she surfed the Internet frequently and played online games, she refused to communicate with them (mostly citing them as shallow and "not Christian"). Anne spoke only to her best friend and neighbor, saying she preferred to "run down the road" to communicate with her. Penelope was a thirteen-year-old from a suburb of New York, whose mother worked in marketing and whose father was a banker, who was beginning to act in school plays and "hang out with the drama kids." She said that she spent at least an hour a night on IM but then did not send me any conversations. Then there was Alex, a fifteen-year-old model from Los Angeles who lived with her father, the CEO of a large company, and stepmother; her mother owned an Internet start-up in another city. Although she seemed to have it made in terms of affluence and beauty, and was allowed to use IM for an hour every night, Alex seemed reserved and awkward and also never sent any conversations or answered later email inquiries.

As thanks for participation, each of the girls in the study received a gift certificate (from $10 to $25, depending on the level of participation) to her choice of Old Navy, Best Buy, or Gap. I also took several of the girls out for pizza as thanks for their interviews.

Instant Identity: An Overview

Viewing IM as a preferred mode of communication among large sectors of adolescent girls, this analysis explores various themes that emerged from the cultural narratives in the girls' conversations and interviews and which are outlined in-depth in each of the chapters. This chapter has outlined the past literature on adolescence, gender, and identity and has provided a cultural context for its place within new media and has explained how I set about my research. Chapter Two discusses not only the importance of IM to an adolescent girl's social world, but it also looks at the many ways the girls in the study used IM to demonstrate social status and, in some cases, "fake" popularity. Conversely, it also looks at how IM may be used for bullying and fighting among girls and investigates the new means of gossip afforded by IM. Although some see IM as simply a version of high-tech note passing, this chapter demonstrates that there is more to it than simple peer-to-peer conversation.

In Chapter Three, IM is viewed as many of the adolescent girls who use it see it—as a private space. Most of the girls in this particular study were allowed to do IM when their parents were not present, and a number of them used computers in spaces that were private from the rest of the household, but all knew the various IM "codes" to alert one another that a parent was present. This was important because not only do their conversations include private revelations and gossip, but they also include a great deal of profanity and vulgarity. The girls also suggest that it was easier to disclose personal feelings online than in person or on the phone, and their IM conversations often cover personal topics such as sexuality and religion. Often, the girls take these private conversations and save or print them to review at a later date—in essence, functioning as an iterative diary of sorts. And much as they would do with a diary, they stressed the importance of hiding these saved conversations from parents and siblings.

Scholars have seen the Internet as a space for articulation of sexual identity (Grisso & Weiss, 2005; Stern, 2002), and Chapter Four discusses how IM is another space within new media where adolescents negotiate sexuality and sexual discourses. Many of the IM conversations included flirtatious conversations between girls and boys—sometimes boyfriends and sometimes simply boys from school whom they hardly knew. In many cases, the language they use is rather sexually forward (whether this is an act of empowerment or "just having fun" is a matter that differs among the girls) or at least hinting that they are "sexy"—at least online. Moreover, a number of the girls converse primarily online with their boyfriends, from hooking up to breaking up, and some say these conversations have drawn them closer. In many of these conversations, it becomes apparent that traditional gender roles are being played out, such as that of a caretaker/mother. This chapter analyzes how these varied understandings of sexuality and gender roles are apparent through IM.

The world of IM is seen as a relatively untapped market where corporations can target youth directly in a space where they spend a large amount of their time. In Chapter Five, I discuss the various marketing tactics deployed by the companies that offer IM devices (primarily including AOL, Yahoo, and Microsoft) and attempt to understand how the use of commercial icons, streaming advertisements, editorial/advertorial marketing reaches (or fails to reach) the girls who use IM. It also discusses the other ways that the companies that deploy IM devices attempt to reach the coveted youth market and how, through various uses of new media, they attempt to sell not only goods, but also, in many cases, identity (through the purchase of goods) to adolescents. The girls' reactions to this advertising and marketing as well as analysis of the corporate messages themselves give a more complete picture of how gender identity may be commodified even in this supposedly "free" space.

Finally, Chapter Six focuses on the implications of IM on adolescent girls, their communication practices, and gender identity. While looking at what these implications say about youth culture in general, it also brings together the theory and themes found throughout the book and discusses specifically why IM is an important factor in gender identity negotiation for girls. It also discusses what this means both now and with regard to the future.

The following chapters will bring you into this world and attempt to argue how it both empowers and confines adolescent girls as they communicate in this new medium. The book demonstrates throughout not only how girls in many ways are postured as the target of corporate messages and dominant cultural discourses that may be harmful to them, but also how they resist these messages and at the same time act as active cultural producers in a medium that are uniquely positioned to understand.

CHAPTER TWO
"How Many Peeps R on 4U?: IM as a Space for Identity Articulation

Within this chapter, I explore the various elements that make IM a free space for identity articulation—a space where the girls who use it feel comfort in confrontation, freedom to use profanity, experimentation with conversational tone, and play with linguistic and grammatical conventions in varying ways. Underlying all of these modes of identity construction is the idea that IM represents a relatively new means for a girl to navigate and the often-rocky social and cultural landscape of modern adolescence.

In this way, adolescent girls' use of IM also demonstrates precisely how technology is socially constructed by its users. Although IM is truly a simple technology that allows users to chat in real time with one another, it is also a means for constructing a social world if you examine the way that many adolescents use it in their daily lives. As they chat with multiple people at the same time, they not only use words to construct identity and make social plans, but they also use silence and other more creative—and sometimes manipulative—forms of both mass and interpersonal communication to create and manage their own social worlds. While some view IM as simply a version of high-tech note passing among teenagers, this chapter demonstrates that there is far more to the practice than many people realize.

Being 'In' on the Language of IM

In the early days of instant-relay chat and Internet chatrooms, adult Internet users invented linguistic shortcuts in their conversations, for example, "lol" meaning laughing out loud or using text characters—or "emoticons"—to signify emotions, such as ☺. Adolescents using IM, however, have taken linguistic shortcuts to an entirely new level in which conversations are somewhat difficult for the average adult to interpret because they use so many abbreviations and emoticons, and often play with the English language in ways that easily upset the average high school English teacher. In all of their interviews, the girls who participated in this research said that they felt IM was something of a free space where they could experiment with different conversational norms than they might use in person. This experimentation not only includes co-opting the "lol" of the early days of the Internet (it appears in many conversations to serve as almost a stock response to a lot of phrases that are not necessarily all that funny), but also the abbreviation of numerous standard phrases. For example, the phrase "not much" is often abbreviated as "nm" and "see you later" is generally written as "c u later." The following conversation is an actual IM conversation between two friends and contains my translation in italics after each phrase, a practice that I will continue throughout the book for readers who do not wish to take the time to decipher the IM language:

Girl2: hey
Girl1: wat *(What?)*
Girl2: nuffi *(Nothing)*
Girl2: u? *(You?)*
Girl2: nm *(Not much.)*
Girl1: who at ur house? *(Who is at your house?)*
Girl2: evan jeff *(Evan and Jeff)*
Girl1: ooo *(Oh)*
Girl2: wat yall doing *(What are you all doing?)*
Girl1: not a damn thing
Girl2: lol *(Laugh out loud)*

Not only do the conversational norms of IM among adolescents challenge the conventions of their English classes, but they also create an "in-group" mentality, in which those who converse are expected to adhere to the norms and in many ways subtly articulate their belonging to the group by using them. Language constructs social meaning among youth peer groups and it can mark distinctions among different cliques and groups as much as language marks distinctions among generations (Eckert, 2005). Many scholars believe that when studied from an intergroup perspective, language norms can explain some very complicated notions of behavior and psychology (Fortman, 2003). In their interviews, girls admitted that this concept holds as true within the world of IM as it holds in their lives in the real world. Girls who do not adhere to the language norms of IM could be seen as outliers—perhaps someone who "thinks she's better than other people or smarter than them," according to Leanne. Similarly, the girls in this book often made fun of adults (like myself) who used perfect grammar with punctuation and capitalization in their IM conversations. However, in some cases, they attempted to adhere to a more formal way of speaking, and they said that they tried to do this when they communicated with adults in writing or worked on school projects. Still, one parent of the daughters who participated in the book said he noticed the IM abbreviations sneaking in to his daughter's printed notes left throughout the house. "Just the other day, I got a note that I literally had to translate," he said. "It was something like, 'Gone 2 JL's house. C-U IALB!'" (He said he believed she meant, "Gone to Jill Lopez's house. See you in a little bit!")

The linguistic conventions expressed in IM go beyond simple abbreviations and manipulation of language and into the realm of profanity and vulgarity. IM conversations submitted by the girls were peppered with both minor profanity (such as "damn," in the above conversation) to much more elevated levels of vulgarity both from them and the persons with whom they conversed. When I asked about their use of profanity in IM, the girls interviewed for this book said they were unlikely to swear out loud or in face-to-face conversations with peers for fear of being caught by a parent or adult but that swearing was simply another language convention associated with IM.

"When i swear online its cause the peeps i talk to are my friends ... otherwize they tick me off, and when i do cuss offline its cause i like drop sumthin or get angry about something," Leanne wrote in an IM conversation with me. When I asked whether she worried about being caught using profanity online, she said she did not but admitted that she did worry the language could carry over into the offline realm. She wrote, "cause online you can x out of da convo and it will clear it and off line they have whats called ears."[4]

An interesting example of excessive profanity is found in a conversation sent by Jordan. As she conversed with friends from school in the conversation that follows this paragraph, she became frustrated with a particular topic she did not understand (in this case, her friends referred to their "Xangas," a brand name for personal Weblogs or blogs that are widely used among adolescents to publish their thoughts to a Web page). In order to get their attention when they ignored her question about Xanga, you can see that she used the same profane phrase over and over again as a humorous means to get attention and force interruption in the ongoing conversation. Here is an excerpt of the conversation sent by Jordan, whose log-in name is starchicachic: who do not wish to take the time to decipher the IM language:

kittyBUTTERfly: u hacked into my xanga!!!
starchicachic: whao
starchicachic: cool

starchicachic: how?

FunMegan88: http://www.xanga.com/home.aspx?user=panonymous

kittyBUTTERfly: NOT KUL!

FunMegan88: now go

starchicachic: i can't

starchicachic: doin hw

FunMegan88: wha/??/

FunMegan88: thats mine

starchicachic: im confuzzled

kittyBUTTERfly: http://www.xanga.com/private/home.aspx.

kittyBUTTERfly: this one is mine

kittyBUTTERfly: u hacker!!!!!!

starchicachic: did u kno dat da worst curse in arabic means literally "your mothers cunt"?

starchicachic: thats the 1 on mine

starchicachic: did u kno dat da worst curse in arabic means literally "your mothers cunt"?

Jordan, who said in her interview that she rarely, if ever, uses profanity aloud in real life, and generally "tries to be good," and has a strong relationship with her parents, reiterated the curse phrase four more times within the rest of the conversation with her friends. Within this conversation, she not only demonstrates a resistance to her friends' ignoring her question by using one of the most profane words she can think of, but she also demonstrates a resistance to the "nice girl" identity that she tries to fit in real life with her parents and at school.

The following conversation between Beth, whose log-in name is Bethybeth, and a classmate represents a more typical, casual use of profanity within conversation. The girls discuss a classmate with whom they are annoyed.

Olive2Kiss: mr bethel told us that the top two throwers would compete on mon so ashley and I are

Bethybeth: wow!!!!

Olive2Kiss: alli was complaining bout that

Bethybeth: why

Bethybeth:: she fucking sucks!!!!

Olive2Kiss: cause i think that she wanted to throw

Olive2Kiss: i no
Bethybeth: i'm sorry but i fucking hate her
Olive2Kiss: !!!!!!!!!!!!!!!!!!1
Olive2Kiss: she pisses me off to

In the previous conversation, Beth and Olive each casually swore in their discussion of the behavior of a girl on their track team. When I asked Beth whether she would have used this kind of language in person, she said she would have done so if she was out of earshot of her coach or other adults, and that she occasionally used profanity among friends. She also acknowledged that she liked how IM allowed her to vent her frustrations and get feedback from another teammate who appeared to share her frustration. Each girl acknowledged that she wrote differently when communicating with adults both by abandoning some abbreviations and slang terms and by writing in complete sentences (in the example of Leanne's response to my question about swearing, she used slang and abbreviations, but she did appear to attempt to write in complete sentences). Although none of the girls articulated IM specifically as a space where they purposely experimented with identity and tone, it seems that the girls are well aware that IM is a space free from the intervention of adults where they have the power to make, adhere to, and enforce their own tacit rules and where they can cast off their good girl identity.

Social Planning through IM

In the past, a simple phone call could confirm a sleepover or a trip to the movies, but now IM has replaced the phone as the chief method of social planning among adolescents. Not only does IM have the advantage of not tying up the phone line,[5] but it also has the added benefit of allowing one to easily contact a number of friends, either through a chatroom-style IM conversation or by quickly navigating through multiple IM windows, a common practice among adolescents IMing.

Not all of the conversations on IM are about secret plans but rather are about social networking and simple day-to-day planning, including discussions of ride sharing, issues with homework, and girls wondering what time after-school events were starting and whether their friends would be showing up at all. For example, Jordan and a friend check in with one another to see whether they are both attending a religion class:

Marcus89: hey
starchicachic: hey
starchicachic: r u goin to hebrew?
Marcus89: yup
starchicachic: oic
Marcus89: are you?
starchicachic: probli *(probably)*

Furthermore, IM provided some of the girls in this book with a silent method of making plans to which parents might object. For example, in one late-night conversation that is not included in this chapter, fifteen-year-old Caitlyn's boyfriend planned to sneak over to her window that night, and in another, which will be included in the next chapter, fifteen-year-old Sunny planned a clandestine date with an older boy from school whom she barely knew. Conversations like these are riddled with sudden "g2g" messages, which means "got to go" often in response to parents entering the room or calling them.

Aggression and Fighting through IM: Not Necessarily Just "Mean Girls"
In the following conversation, Nicole demonstrates not only all of the elements that make IM a free space for identity articulation—comfort in confrontation, freedom to use profanity, experimentation with conversational tone, and play with linguistic and grammatical conventions—but she also demonstrates another common theme within IM: girls fighting—and not in the backbiting, gossipy way described by the literature on "mean girls" (Simmons, 2002; Talbot, 2002), but rather in an overtly violent way that is usually associated with boys. Nicole, whose log-in for this conversation is a vulgar phrase that can be interpreted loosely as "your boyfriend is in love with me," fought in this conversation with a friend named Devin who believed Nicole stole her boyfriend. The fight also centers on Devin's "profile."[6] Here, Nicole, whose log-in name is junkytrunk16, accused Devin, whose log-in name is babyfizzle, of writing mean-spirited gossip about Nicole and her friend, Aza, in her profile.

> **junkytrunk16:** devin dat was real fowl wat u had in ur profile earlier *(devin, that was real foul what you had in your profile earlier)*
> **junkytrunk16:** sayiin BITCHES these days ppl *(people)* need 2 grow up or wateva *(whatever)*

babyfizzle: yea well ur cruddy and so is aza, and thats how i feel so oh well

junkytrunk16: how am i crddy 2 any1 *(cruddy to anyone)*

babyfizzle: :-/

junkytrunk16: an dif sum1 was 2 call u a bitch u wuld be quick 2 fight them devin

babyfizzle: lest not forget how u said u aint have my back bf, i act like these thing dont bother me but they do and im mad

babyfizzle: lets* *(the asterisk was inserted by Devin, but appears to have no real meaning)*

Cultural models are "tools of inquiry" that people use to mediate between institutional meanings and personal, culturally situated meanings—and they are often expressed through interaction with others (Gee, 1999, p. 58). The ease with which girls may use profanity in the absence of parents and other authority figures is pertinent in a discussion of relevant cultural models within IM. In defining cultural models, it is important to answer the question of what feelings, values, conscious, and unconscious beliefs are apparent within the conversations, and in these particular conversations, the ease with which girls seem to transgress the hegemonic cultural models of femininity is vital. Girls in past studies adhered to a cultural expectation for niceness not just among adults but among other peers (Brown & Gilligan, 1992; Finders, 1996; Orenstein, 1994; Pipher, 1994). Because of unstated societal expectation that girls fit into unattainable models of perfection—from body size to politeness and even deference to male peers—the girls in these studies often took extreme measures to suppress negative or aggressive feelings and outward manifestations of these feelings. This longing to be the "perfect girl" appears to be changing in more recent literature that paints modern girls as catty and aggressive with one another (Lamb, 2001; Simmons, 2002; Talbot, 2002). The strain of profanity and aggression found in these IM conversations (which are entirely between and among females only) not only flouts traditional standards of femininity, but might also seem to exemplify a new way in which girls have embraced meanness with one another. As the IM fight carries on, it is clear that neither girl falls into authors' newer constructions of girls as quietly manipulative or mean (Lamb, 2001; Simmons, 2002; Talbot, 2002). These girls, both of whom are African American in this case and use a racial epithet within the conversation, very directly confront one another in this conversation, and threaten physical violence:

babyfizzle: yea i would fight

babyfizzle: so?

junkytrunk16: devin u were boutta *(about to)* fight over Darren

babyfizzle: niga

junkytrunk16: that dont matter

junkytrunk16: wat do look like fight 4 a boy especially a boy dat aint mine

junkytrunk16: AND

junkytrunk16:L we heard 1st that we were gettin jumped

junkytrunk16: u wanted 2 fight dat gurl on ur own she didnt wanna fight u dat was ur choice

babyfizzle: w/e *(whatever)* Nicole

junkytrunk16: man devin ur really actin dumb bout dis

junkytrunk16: but w/e then

babyfizzle: im actin dumb?

junkytrunk16: i never did nuttiin 2 u so take it like u want it

babyfizzle: wtf *(what the fuck)*

babyfizzle: young Nicole

junkytrunk16: wat

babyfizzle: shut the fuck up for real, ur stupid as h ell just shut up

junkytrunk16: how am i stupid

babyfizzle: no i kno dat ur gettin mad at me 4 nuttin

The following conversation between Beth and Olive also suggests physical violence, even though it is they who talk about it rather nonchalantly, which in many ways suggests Beth—who had been a victim of bullying in the past—attempting to construct her identity as more aggressive and tough than she might be perceived in real life.

Olive2Kiss: mr butz told us that the top two throwers would compete on mon so ashley and I are

Bethybeth: wow!!!!

Olive2Kiss: megan was complaining bout that

Bethybeth: why

Bethybeth: she fucking sucks!!!!

Olive2Kiss: cause i think that she wanted to throw

Olive2Kiss: i no

Bethybeth: i'm sorry but i fucking hate her

Olive2Kiss: !!!!!!!!!!!!!!!!!!!1

Olive2Kiss: she pisses me off to

Olive2Kiss: i don't even talk to her nemore

Olive2Kiss: i would say hi and nice throw and everythin but i cant do that anymore

Bethybeth: why

Olive2Kiss: cause she lost all respect when she left w/the shots and discusses and told mr buts that she gave them to one of us so we got in troble for it and then we had to look for them so we made all of the other teams wait cause they wouldn't justleave one bus behind

Olive2Kiss: *trouble

Bethybeth: i would have fucking chewed her ass in front of everyone and then beat her up

Olive2Kiss: lol

Bethybeth: no joke

Olive2Kiss: o i forgot bout kickin emily's ass

Bethybeth: i know!!!!!

Bethybeth: omg *(oh my god)*

Bethybeth: now she completely denies everything she did to me!!!!!!

Bethybeth: shes really askin for it!

Olive2Kiss: yes she is

Bethybeth: what did she do to you?

Olive2Kiss: she slapped me to

Bethybeth: omg

Olive2Kiss: she isnt cool

Olive2Kiss: or funny

Dominant notions of femininity still suggest that young girls should be more hesitant to broach delicate matters in as confrontational a manner as male peers, suggesting that girls are, at best, "natural" mediators, and, at worst, unlikely leaders. IM appears to provide an outlet in which girls may be as direct and confrontational as they like. In their interviews the girls said that, in general, they felt more comfortable conversing via IM than in face-to-face or phone conversation (although they often did both, sometimes using the phone as a follow-up, or speaking on the phone with another friend while conducting the IM fight with an adversary). In another conversation, Beth's sister Leanne confronted a classmate over a misunderstanding that occurred at an after-school basketball practice. In a follow-up interview, Leanne said she probably would have ignored "stjamesgirl" and given her "dirty looks" had she not been able to reach her via IM; instead, this IM confrontation cleared up the misunderstanding, said Leanne, whose log-in name is "Leanne is SEXY!!!":

> **stjamesgirl:** hey
> **Leanne is SEXY!!!:** what is up
> **stjamesgirl:** nothing
> **Leanne is SEXY!!!:** y did you say that our team sucks?
> **stjamesgirl:** hey who are you talking to and what are you talking about
> **stjamesgirl**: your team members
> **stjamesgirl:** hey what are you talking about at the game cause ya I said that they suck casue i go t mad that we lost or won my name I just meeten *(meant)* that we werent the only team that sucks so our teams suck to
> **Leanne is SEXY!!!:** OK
> **stjamesgirl:** K

Although Lindsay did not display the overt aggression with Tyler that the girls in the previous conversations demonstrated with each other, she was able to confront a troubling situation head on through IM rather than wonder who was spreading unflattering gossip about her. Although she might have confronted him in person, she said she felt that IM provided a much easier venue for articulating her feelings and to enable her to stay collected.

Faking Popularity and Articulating Social Standing through IM

In the world of IM, social standing may be linked to identity construction in ways not seen in the concrete hallways of middle schools and high schools in past history. Online, the process of constructing oneself is simple and may be done in a variety of ways: lying (e.g., telling someone that you are not wearing clothing when in fact you are); using technology to manipulate conversation (e.g., pretending the computer is not working when in fact you are ignoring another person's attempt to contact you); changing tone to manipulate conversation (e.g., using a lot of profanity and exclamation points to convey an angrier tone and, potentially, to incite fear); and simply disclosing information about oneself that makes a particular impression (e.g., if a girl says that she has been invited to several upcoming slumber parties, there is no one there to interrupt and deny it). In this study, I identified the girls' attention to maintaining or constructing popularity within the use of IM as an "ideational code" (Lindlof, 1995, p. 220). By detecting popularity and acceptance as "subjects that are dramatized by the participants, or that are glossed by them" (Lindlof, 1995, p. 220), I learned that social standing—although rarely mentioned explicitly in the girls' interviews or directly broached in their conversations—is an important part of the reason they use IM.

These girls used IM conversations to elevate their social standing in many interesting ways, a finding that is consistent with Lewis and Fabos's study (2000) of adolescent girls and IM. Through the manipulation of tone and selective disclosure about themselves, they attempted to control conversation and present themselves in a positive light. For example, they disclosed private information, such as information about certain boys being interested in them. They also disclosed more status-driven information, sometimes bragging about accomplishments and about consumer goods that they either purchased or received from parents. An example is found in a conversation in which Beth told a friend she had been chosen to compete as a primary discus thrower at an upcoming track meet. She also talked about a fashionable new watch she had just purchased and bragged about how she intended to beat up another girl in her class for spreading gossip about her.

Furthermore, in interviews, the girls often bragged about how many conversations they could hold at a given time; although none of them explicitly told me they did this to instill a sense of self-satisfaction, they clearly appeared to be somewhat proud of this fact. The girls mentioned that they would hold IM conversations with as many people as possible in a given amount of time, usually simultaneously. Their "buddy lists," a listing of people's log-in names that allows them to see who is online at a given time, contained as many as fifty other friends with whom they regularly chatted and in some cases many other names of people whose log-in names they had obtained through camp or extracurricular activities but whom they rarely saw offline or communicated with online. In one conversation, Beth actually asked a friend[7] how many people she was talking to at a given moment and who they are:

Carolinesweety: whos on for u?

Bethybeth: um.. lemme check

Bethybeth: anne, bethany jack,carna,u,colleen,amy,mandy ,an my cuzs friend

Carolinesweety: sh except i have more *(SH means "Same here")*

Bethybeth: like who??

Carolinesweety: jeff, Dylan, chris, carrie and alotmorw

Carolinesweety: and jack

Bethybeth: how many peeps r on?? *(how many people are on?)*

Carolinesweety: 10

Bethybeth: ic

Some of the girls who participated in the research for this book also used IM essentially to "fake" popularity. In attempts to "appear" socially unavailable, girls admitted to taking extra time before answering messages—even if they were not busy—to give the illusion that they were busy chatting with other friends. (This might be akin to answering the phone on the third ring to make one seem less anxious about receiving a call or waiting a day or two after a good date to call to ask for another date.) Similar to girls interviewed by Lewis and Fabos (2000) who demonstrated how they waited at least several seconds before answering certain IMs, the girls in my study admitted to doing the same often. Caitlyn went further: "Sometimes it's just best to wait awhile before writing back so you can discourage certain people from talking to you at all."

Although using IM to construct self in the eyes of peers was common, I should note that one girl in particular explained that she would not use IM because she viewed it as an extension of the more unfortunate parts of teenage social life. Anne, a fourteen-year-old daughter of a Methodist minister and stay-at-home mom from rural Iowa, said in her interview that she found the world of IM that preoccupied the time of her classmates as "shallow." She said that although her family had an Internet connection that was used for schoolwork and online gaming, she specifically avoided IM because it was associated with the social world of peers whom she did not like and, in many cases, did not like her. "The only person that I want to talk to is my friend, Josie, who lives down the road, and if I want to talk to her, I can run down the road," said Anne. "I don't feel like there's any reason for me to IM anyone who I go to school with." Anne, in this regard, resists certain cultural models that seem to be at work within the online and offline lives of most of her peers—most notably, the belief that IM will assist in elevating her social status or even the notion that she would want to elevate her social status at all. Although this appears to be an unusual finding within the interviews and IM conversations of most of the girls in the study, it is important to ask questions about how her self-imposed exclusion from the

IM network (which she has chosen) is played out in terms of identity articulation. According to Anne herself, the choice to not use IM did not play into any overall issues with socialization or identity articulation, and although I was not able to observe her peer reactions in a school setting, I was able to spend time with her at a summer journalism workshop where she socialized and spent time with the "popular" adolescents in her group and appeared to be quite self-aware and adjusted. The choice to exclude herself from IM conversations and cliques might be akin to Merskin's analysis of "Jammer Girls," who "choose, in healthy ways, to reject the confines of good- versus bad-girl femininity" (Merskin, 2005, p. 57), only in Anne's case, she might do so by *avoiding* the often "shallow" conversations her peers shared online than by embracing the medium as a place to articulate and construct her personal identity.

Although Anne said that in choosing to avoid IM she avoided people with whom she did not want to associate, other girls in the study said they felt that classmates who did not participate in IM socialization might be at a social disadvantage. In an email follow-up interview, Lindsay said socializing for such girls is, at the very least, slowed down. "While I don't think it really affects them in that I don't think they are looked down on for not using IM, I do think that it puts them at a disadvantage because it allows a person to talk to many people all at one time," she wrote. "And especially to find something to do at nights ... it seems like everyone is on the computer in late afternoons and night and it's more convenient to see what is all going on."

IM as a Means of Social Exclusion

In their interviews, the girls admitted to sometimes using the technology to manipulate conversations. As Caitlyn mentioned previously, she might "discourage" certain people from IMing her by being slow to answer their messages. Or more overtly, they might "block" someone, and not admit to doing so if confronted about it later. This particular technological feature is very helpful in keeping away unwanted advances from strangers (an issue that a few of the girls addressed, saying that occasionally a stranger would somehow get their log-in name and attempt to contact them), but it can be used to assist in managing one's social life as well. While "blocking" may be used as a means to elevate and articulate social identity among the adolescents using IM, it is also used for more deleterious purposes. In the course of the study, Beth was a victim of being "blocked" by all of her eighth-grade classmates. The blocking took place offline as well as online as she noted her peers had started excluding her at recess, not inviting her to birthday parties, and making snide comments as they passed her in the hallway. Although she said she felt "angry" and "like a loser" because of what was going on both at school and online, Beth also said she felt thankful her classmates had not resorted to harassing her via IM by signing up for fake screen names and taunting her. Only one other girl in the study mentioned the practice of signing up for "extra" IM accounts for the purpose of sending anonymous messages to people, but Beth said that two other girls from school had been harassed in this manner and that each stopped using IM altogether after the incidents.

Indeed, social exclusion among adolescents is an age-old problem. Despite the Internet's early promises of empowerment—particularly for women and girls who could use the technology to achieve cultural power that might not have been possible in past situations (Haraway, 1991)—the Internet, and IM specifically, is another popular tool for exclusion. Some research shows that girls frequently bully within tightly knit networks of friends and make the aggression less physical and, thus, more difficult for authority figures to identify, as opposed to boys who often act out their aggression physically and do not appear to do so based on peer group standing but because of an escalating verbal confrontation (Simmons, 2002). Moreover, girls who previously fought using silence and exclusion or spreading vicious gossip may seize upon IM as a way to freeze conversation with certain individuals or spread rumors within their social networks at a pace that is not possible in person (Talbot, 2002). Though those who spread gossip and manipulate conversation through IM articulate identity in very public ways, questions must be raised about how identity is negotiated by the girls who have in effect been silenced and whether the silencing is good in that it encourages them to navigate the social system differently in more positive ways, or whether it may simply cause the girls to feel excluded and alienated.

IM and Gossip

Teenagers have been known stereotypically to hang on the telephone for hours on end, mastering their social lives and venting their feelings to friends and, in essence, negotiating private and social connections in a disembodied communication medium. Martin, in her ethnographic cultural history of the telephone (1991), says adult women telephone users (through person-to-person conversation and also through the rural party-line system that used to be prevalent in the United States and Canada) developed a culture of the telephone. The women appropriated the telephone, which was developed with businessmen in mind, to suit their own social needs and, in turn, created their own space for socialization and community. Prior to this appropriation, Martin writes, the telephone's initial public perception initially positioned it as a technology that made its users nervous because of their fear of being unable to use it properly, but the women ultimately found the phone to be empowering. Despite its technologically empowering qualities, the telephone was positioned instead as a gendered technology that perpetuates the sexist stereotype of women as gossips even into modern times (Martin, 1991).

Rakow (1992) also used an ethnographic approach to study the gendered use of the telephone, acknowledging from the outset of her research that women's dependence on the telephone signified isolation and loneliness that must be questioned in "a changing Western landscape of public and private spheres" (Rakow, 1992, p. 211). Arguing that the telephone functions not as a neutral technology but as a gendered technology or a "site of which the meanings of gender are expressed and practiced" (Rakow, 1992, p. 33), Rakow asserts that women's telephone use "is both *gendered* work—work delegated to women—and *gender* work—work that confirms the community's beliefs about what are women's natural tendencies and abilities" (p. 33, emphasis added). Concluding that the telephone is a "symptom, possibility, weapon, companion, tool, and lifeline" (p. 154), Rakow calls upon feminist scholars to question why such a potentially empowering technology has yet to transform current social practices for women, and instead is viewed as a mechanism for gossip and marginalized as a social tool for "woman talk" (p. 36). More recently, Kearney (2005) analyzed the association between teenage girls and social progress and reinforcement of patriarchy as symbolized through their growing use of the telephone in the twentieth century. As a signifier of modern girlhood in the 1940s through early 1960s in the United States, she said that the telephone demonstrated how girls could be liberated from the domestic sphere by being allowed to communicate with the outside world at their own will and at the same time, how it still confined them to the home because that was the only place that telephone conversations could take place in that era.

IM already has gained a reputation as a gendered technology where gossip and "girl talk" prevail. In two recent studies (AOL/DMS, 2004; Tufte, 2003, p. 72), adolescent girls were found to be the primary users because they like to chat and "converse with family and friends" (http://www.aolepk.com/red/fact_sheet.html) whereas boys used the Internet to play games. This statistic somewhat essentializes the gendered split positioning of boys as fierce competitors and girls as friendly negotiators. Looking at how women's ability to communicate and men's ability to compete have been constructed in the history of the workplace and upper levels of education, this gendered split ultimately could be harmful to girls as they may not be viewed as capable of competing in the marketplace as their male peers (Gilligan, 1982). This book by no means wishes to further paint girls as petty gossips, and the following sections will demonstrate to a certain degree how girls transgress the cultural stereotype in IM and resist the discourses traditionally associated with girls and communication.

Still, IM raises interesting new issues about spreading gossip. With space and time so constrained by technology, it is much easier to spread rumors more quickly among a large group of people than it would be in person, by mail or email, or by telephone. Words are often misunderstood when typed on a screen—certain inflections are missing and people may misinterpret information being passed along to them. Moreover, because IM is essentially a written medium, it also provides an uncomplicated way of spreading gossip by allowing users to cut and paste conversations with others and send them to others via IM. The following is a conversation between fifteen-year-old Emma from Louisiana and her classmate Lisa who sent Emma a conversation that recently had been sent to Lisa from another classmate. The conversation that is pasted here is between two other girls in her class who fought using not only malicious verbal barbs against one another but also accused each other of questionable behaviors:

LisaJ: hahah look
LisaJ: this is between sarah and jc
LisaJ: sarah used to be my bff *(best friend forever)* but now its jc
LisaJ: its funny look
Emma: lol
(LisaJ pastes conversation, which was sent to her by another friend)
sarahjj: i could careless what yall fuckin do .. your so fucked up in   the head

sarahjj: the last thing i am is jealous

sarahjj: i have friends....

jc: oooooo IM fucked up in the head? oh plz sarah ur the biggest fuck up ever ur so insecure about urself u   have to go around fucking guys and popping pills

sarahjj: its over

sarahjj: bye

jc: oo ur such a lil hoe u cant defend urself now

jc: i just wanna fight

sarahjj: bitch bring it

(back to original conversation between Lisa and Emma)

LisaJ: hahahahah

LisaJ: and im missing this!

Emma: funny shit

LisaJ: i know

This conversation also suggests a blurring of public and private space within IM that is not apparent within other modes of communication. Because of the prevalence of cutting and pasting within IM conversations shared with peers, those conversing must be aware that all that they write— even the private conversations—might be shared with many others afterward. Although more conniving IM users could use this technical innovation as a means for spreading false gossip (in other words, making up and typing a fake conversation using another person's log-in name and typing something that she might not normally say), in their interviews, the girls each said that they did not know of such cases. They said that they generally assumed that if a conversation was pasted and sent to them by a friend, the content would be trustworthy.

However, the older girls participating in the research for this book said that they thought more carefully about what they wrote within their IM conversations because of fear of their conversations getting reproduced (each suspected this had happened to them in the past but had no concrete proof), which is a consistent finding in other interviews with girls who use IM (Clark, 2005). In most cases, the girls felt that pasted IM conversations were strong affirmations that the gossip was actually true. For example, in the following conversation, fifteeen-year-old Lindsay learns from a friend that a boy whom she likes also has a crush on her, and the friend— Dana6fouryou—verifies the information by pasting an IM conversation with the boy in question (as a note further emphasizing how quickly gossip may be spread by IM, the friend is IMing the boy at the same time that she is IMing Lindsay):

> **Dana6fouryou:** matt thinks your cute
> **sportzwoman:** smith???
> **Dana6fouryou:** yea lol!!
> **Dana6fouryou:** he likes you a lot
> **sportzwoman:** yeah he doesn't
> **Dana6fouryou:** no for real
> **sportzwoman:** send me ur convo
> **sportzwoman:** Pleaz
> **Dana6fouryou:** yea
> **Dana6fouryou:** Here it is *(conversation is pasted here)*
> **Matt smith:** know who i kinda like.........
> **Dana6fouryou:** who is that???
> **Matt smith:** Lindsay
> **Dana6fouryou:** awwwwww
> **Matt smith:** but i doubt she would EVER go for me!
> *(return to original conversation)*
> **sportzwoman:** lol thats funny
> **Dana6fouryou:** he really likes you
> **sportzwoman:** o my
> **sportzwoman:** that's funny
> **Dana6fouryou:** *(accidentally hitting "enter" or conveying silence)*
> **Matt smith:** tell her, im serious
> **sportzwoman:** lol, are u sending our messages back and forth??? lol lol lol lol
> **Dana6fouryou:** not yours cause there all disses
> **sportzwoman:** did u send that to him??
> **sportzwoman:** lol
> **Dana6fouryou:** hahah yea

An almost-identical conversation takes place between Sunny and a male friend who has a crush on her. When Sunny, whose log-in name is firekiss23, accuses the male friend, whose log-in name is mynameisj, of liking her sister, rather than telling her directly, he uses a conversation between himself and Sunny's sister to let her know that he likes Sunny instead:

firekiss23: yea. sooo do u lik emy sis? u look like u do. LOL

mynameisj: what

mynameisj: i like the other sis though

firekiss23: o really? wat's her name?

mynameisj: what u think how many sisters are there

firekiss23: like 5

mynameisj: no only 2

firekiss23: hehe yup. so u like me? Lol

mynameisj: ru the other sister

firekiss23: i think so...

mynameisj: hehe. yea. anywayz –

(mynameisj *pastes a conversation he had with Sunny's sister, Jamie, here*)

Jamie12: i think ur really shy

Jamie12: just tell her u like her

Jamie12: and u want ta go out w her

Jamie12: and y wanna kiss her and hug her

(back to original conversation with Sunny and Joshua)

firekiss23: OMG!!!! *(Oh my God!)*

firekiss23: wth *(what the hell)*

firekiss23: my sis is sooo weird!!

mynameisj: nah

mynameisj: shes telling the truth

firekiss23: fo real??

mynameisj: yea

mynameisj: ill ttyl aight *(I'll talk to you later, all right?)*

firekiss23: aight *(all right)*

Although neither of the latter conversations blatantly excludes the others, the parties who are quoted within them (Matt Smith, the boy with a crush on Lindsay, and Jamie, Sunny's sister) stand to be somewhat embarrassed by what they wrote whereas the girls forwarding the messages appear to show no remorse or embarrassment for sharing the information. This somewhat disputes the gendered notions of girls and gossips: Historically, girls who are "gossips" have been characterized as unmannerly and, therefore, girls who spread gossip do so in secret; in IM, this appears to have changed because the gossip is so easily traced. However, in a conversation later in the evening, Lindsay actually sent an IM to Matt Smith, letting him know that her friend told her that he liked her; while Smith seemed slightly embarrassed by the disclosure, he joked about it in the IM conversation and welcomed the opportunity to ask Lindsay out.

Matt smith: u got all that?
sportzwoman: lol
Matt smith: since u know, what do u think
sportzwoman: idk (I don't know)
sportzwoman: its cool
sportzwoman: im flattered
Matt smith: whew
Matt smith: so?
sportzwoman: so what?
Matt smith: wanna go to a movie
sportzwoman: OK, sometime…

When I interviewed Sunny about the conversation between her sister and the male friend that was forwarded to her, she said that her sister also was not upset by having her conversation forwarded to Sunny and, in fact, expected it. It seems that IM users are aware of the consequences of easy disclosure and constant surveillance by their peers, and they continue to disclose personal information and feelings on IM regardless of potential embarrassment or hurt feelings.

This brings into question the notion of how the constant surveillance afforded by IM may affect the lives of those who use it. It seems from their reflections on their IM use that the girls studied for this book are aware of the consequences that may arise from their performance online, and yet they continue to disclose personal information and feelings on IM regardless of potential embarrassment or hurt feelings. Though the person initially writing the message is most likely conveying truthful information that they realize might be passed along to others, she generally appears to understand that in the culture of her social group, it is acceptable for peers to paste and share conversations with others. The girls in this book appeared to acquiesce to this notion, often taking some advantage of the situation, such as in the case of Lindsay's friend nudging Matt Smith into making a date with Lindsay.

Further, this practice demonstrates the true lack of clarity between what constitutes private space versus public space in the use of IM. Although the conversations between and among its participants are often considered "private," those writing tend to realize the ease with which these private conversations can become public knowledge.

Although the idea that private conversations can so easily be shared may be disturbing to adults, this blurring of private and public space or private and public information is less of an issue to this generation of girls. Clark (2005) wrote the adolescents in this "constant contact generation" value control over their social environments (e.g., through IM, email, and cell phone exchanges) so much that certain personal disclosures are often worth the social risk:

> On the one hand, it holds for young women the promise of being able to manage relationships through their written communication skills, which are generally better than those of their male counterparts. Yet on the other hand, the normalizing of such constant contact means the ever-present worry of needing to perform oneself appropriately, and the twin need to be constantly evaluated as acceptable, or simply okay, in the context of one's peers. Trust between peers must therefore be negotiated within each instant message, email, text or multimedia message, or cell phone exchange. (pp. 216–217).

Keeping in mind this constant negotiation to which she refers, the following chapter explores how IM—while clearly functioning as a public space—may also function as a venue for private exploration of identity where parents and authority figures are not allowed.

CHAPTER THREE
"I got to intercept that mail before the parental gets home":
Instant Messaging as a Private Space

The first question that most parents and educators ask when the topic of adolescent girls and IM is broached is "Is it safe?" With regular stories in the national news about sexual predators using the Internet to prey on teenagers online and arranging to meet them in person, it may seem as though children are in constant danger. In 1999, a study commissioned by the National Center for Missing and Exploited Children found that one in five children reported having received a sexual approach or solicitation when they were online over that past year, an alarming statistic that has no follow-up numbers for more recent years. In 2001, the Pew Center for Internet and American Life found that 52 percent of adolescents "do not worry at all" about being approached by strangers online (57 percent of parents report that they are worried about it) (Lenhart et al., 2001). This disconnect is interesting, particularly because most teens in the Pew survey said they IM only with people whom they or their friends know. The girls interviewed for this book said the same, and most of them avoided chat rooms entirely, which is a consistent finding in other studies of adolescents and the Internet (Clark, 2005; Lewis & Fabos, 2000). Parents recently have become more vigilant about their children's activities online, specifically worrying about whether they are speaking with strangers and disclosing personal information (Lenhart, 2005), a finding consistent with what the girls in this book said.

"My mom always thinks I'm talking to strangers and not people I know and see all the time," said Nicole, from the DC suburbs. However, Nicole viewed IM as a safe space in her life because it allowed her the opportunity to privately converse with friends and articulate her feelings. Even though the computer was located in her mother's bedroom and her mother regularly checked in on her when she used the Internet,[9] Nicole said she felt the computer still provided a haven for communication she did not have in the offline world because it was not possible for her parents or teachers to eavesdrop on what she said. This idea that the Internet provides a safe space for self-expression and disclosure has been explored in past literature on adolescents and new media by examining the Web pages that they publish and the topics they explore on those pages (Mazzarella, 2005; Stern, 1999, 2002) and the online forums in which they participate and both share and gain personal information (Churcher, 2006; Grisso & Weiss, 2005; Tobin, 1998).

In many ways, however, even with the computer residing in a location that is open to other family members, IM is a private space where parents are shut out of their teens' lives, often in a very physical, literal way that can make parents feel like their adolescent is far from under their watchful eyes. The very act of using IM is silent, consisting only of a single adolescent typing on a keyboard, so no one can overhear the conversation. The IM window can be easily and quickly closed if someone intrudes into the physical space. It is possible to keep a "log" of IM messages with some IM programs, but this may seem like a serious breech of privacy, especially for parents of older teens who value that privacy above all else. Besides, many parents do not have the technical expertise to figure out how to access the logs of their teens' IM conversations, and in many ways, this gap between the generations in technical expertise can place even further space between adolescents and parents in that the latter feel they are unable to supervise their children because they do not have the same level of knowledge about the technology (Leonardi, 2003; Livingstone, 2002; Ribak, 2001)

Many adolescents acknowledge that unsupervised space is an attractive advantage of using IM, as is exemplified in the profanity that many use when IMing with friends. And although the idea of IM serving as a private space away from authority tends to trouble parents for many understandable reasons, it provides a relatively safe environment where adolescents can experiment with identity and articulate themselves as they straddle the worlds of childhood and adulthood.

Instant Messaging as a Private Space

Although most of the girls in the study said that parents were present or nearby when they did much of the IMing with friends, all knew the various IM "codes" to alert one another that a parent was present such as brb for "be right back" or mh for "Mom's here." In addition to hiding any embarrassing disclosures or uses of profanity, the girls also suggested that keeping their conversations private made it easier for them to discuss personal and often embarrassing topics over IM.

More upsetting to parents, however, would be the idea that a number of girls agreed that IM provided an outstanding place to hide information from their parents. For example, in this conversation, Emma discussed her plunging grades and plans to remove her negative progress report from the mailbox before her dad could see it:

Emma: whats the status of ur math grad? *(what's the status of your math grade?)*
S: still an F
Emma: yeh same w/ English *(Yeah, same with English)*
Emma: what kind of F?
S: 64
S: what about your F?
Emma: not bad, i have a 56
Emma: but hey i had a 36 last week so thats pretty good i raised it fast
S: not good
Emma: and he is givin me a chance to make up all my grammar and vocab quizzes that i didnt take cuz i was absent and i got a 0 for ti and so i can make it up before the weekend *(And he is giving me a chance to make up all my grammar and vocabulary quizzes that I didn't take because I was absent and I got a 0 for it, and so I can make it up before the weekend.)*
Emma: but they mailed the progress reports today
S: well that was nice of him
Emma: yeh, hes usually an ass
S: hahahah
Emma: so it will prob. come wednesday, so i got to intercept that mailbefore the parental gets home
Emma: lol so ne ways u think y can pull that up? i think u can *(laugh out loud—so any ways you think you can pull that up? I think you can)*
Emma: my dad was like i don't care if u get a D — as long as u pass lol
Emma: and as long as u dont have to go to sumer skool

In addition to escaping the gaze of their parents, IM can allow adolescent girls to escape the gaze of their peers, which can be desirable for many reasons. For example, IM allows male–female friendships to develop in ways that might not be possible in real life, particularly among younger IM users who still may show disdain toward members of the opposite sex. If caught talking to certain boys in school, Beth said she might be accused of "being his girlfriend," even if she is just being friendly. Moreover, Beth said she feels more comfortable confronting boys in a friendly way via IM because she could speak more freely. "Some things are just too embarrassing to say in real life," she said. The Pew study concurs: 37 percent of the adolescent IM users say they have said something online that they would not have said in person (Lenhart et al., 2001). In the following conversation, she confronted Jonathan, a male friend, about his relationship with one of her best friends—a confrontation she said she would not have had in person because she feared his reaction and the reactions of classmates.

> **Bethybeth:** so whats goin on with u and bridget?
> **Jonathan99:** i dunno
> **Jonathan99:** do u no something that i shoud
> **Bethybeth:** i dont think so besides that fact that u guys are like and never talk to each other
> **Bethybeth:** i think personally u guys communacatied more when u guys werent a couple
> **Jonathan99:** whatever
> **Bethybeth:** whatever my butt

The confrontation is similar to the one in the previous chapter between Lindsay and a boy in her class whom she accused of spreading rumors about her, but, in this case, IM simply allows Beth to approach a member of the opposite sex without feeling the ramifications. Approaching someone and chatting with them over IM simply seemed less personally and socially risky to them, whether it meant speaking more freely to classmates who they did not know well in real life but who they befriended online (some said they spoke primarily to certain people from school only through IM) or to boys in whom they were interested romantically, a topic that will be explored more in the following chapter. In addition, IM provided a venue for friends to discuss their respective crushes without being teased by others around them. For example, in this conversation, Aza and Ally (a fourteen-year-old white classmate of Aza whose log-in is deAllyG3) discuss social plans and the possibility of seeing a boy from school at an evening basketball game:

> **deAllyG3:** u goin2 ur game 2day? *(You going to your game today?)*
> **Aza8:** i dont kno
> **deAllyG3:** oh
> **deAllyG3:** so wsup *(so what's up?)*
> **Aza8:** im chillin

Aza8: is u going?

deAllyG3: i wanted to but i doubt it cuz i dunno where Archibald *(School)* is

Aza8: oo

Aza8: do u kno where maya live?

deAllyG3: yea

deAllyG3: yea

deAllyG3: call him and tell him to give u directions from there

deAllyG3: its not that far

deAllyG3: oh aight lol is he home? *(Oh, aight—slang for all right—laugh out loud, is he home?)*

Aza8: i dont kno

deAllyG3: oh

deAllyG3: he need to stop fakin and talk 2 u

deAllyG3: he is gay

Aza8: so i dont care

deAllyG3: haha but u still got it for him ri *(right)*?

Aza8: yea

Aza8: but i like this other guy

Aza8: to

deAllyG3: awwwwww who do YOU like

Aza8: lo

Aza8: dont tell maya

deAllyG3: i wont gurl i promise

Aza8: cuz they aint great friends

deAllyG3: haha oooohhh

deAllyG3: but i wont tell anyway

Aza8: his name geoff.pronounced jeff

deAllyG3: oh cuz i was liek geoff?? whoah reminded me of giraffe for a sec but aighty *(all righty)* lol

deAllyG3: do he like u?

Aza8: lol

Aza8: yea

Aza8: he do

Aza8: but we gotta get to kno each other more

deAllyG3: tru....u go gurl haha

Aza8: lol

deAllyG3: g2g

Discussion of boys and crushes is hardly surprising private conversational fodder among fourteen-year-old classmates, but the conversation also demonstrates an important phenomenon, as described by Clark (2005) in her analysis of teens and uses of technology: the importance to adolescents that they maintain a sense of power in their uses of new media technology. As is seen in the conversation above, the power is illustrated first by the fact that Aza made social plans that she hoped would involve seeing a boy whom she likes—social plans to which her parents were not privy and, as she signaled by using the "g2g" (got to go) sign when one of them entered the room, she did not intend for them to learn. Second, Aza demonstrated the power to manage and manipulate her social life through IM by discussing a potential new boyfriend and determining with the help of a friend how she might go about seeing him, and, in the process, she ensured that her friend would continue to view her as someone with whom she can share information and more than likely trust. The disclosure signals her conscious choice to pass along private information—knowing the potential consequences of the IM conversation being forwarded to others—and her friend's assurance that she would not tell another mutual friend signaled that they shared a special bond over the secret, private information. This is also seen in an IM conversation that I had with Beth, one of the girls who often shared personal information with me when we chatted (particularly after a time when she was "blocked" by a number of her classmates and instead IMed me to chat through the ordeal). I had IMed her to ask for clarification on some IM conversations that she had sent me earlier that week and she admitted (without any context or provocation) that she was angry with her mother for not driving her into the nearby town for swimming at the city pool.

Bethybeth: i hate my mom
Me: Why? Everything OK?
Bethybeth: no. she wont take me to town and wont let me drive
Me: What is in town? You aren't old enough to drive, are you?
Bethybeth: The pool
Bethybeth: its sooooooooo boring out here!
Bethybeth: i have a permit *(Beth had recently acquired a school permit, but it did not allow her to drive anywhere outside of school and school activities)*
Me: I see

Bethybeth: last summer i rode my bike to Smithville cause my mom wouldnt take me in

Me: wow! That's far!

Bethybeth: so i ran away

Me: where did you go?

Bethybeth: Smithville and i never came home

Me: like to whose house?

Bethybeth: well i went to my s-ball tourny and then i went to my aunts house and stayed over night

Me: at least you were safe

Bethybeth: kinda

Bethybeth: and then i rode back home

Me: That's quite a trip!

Bethybeth: my mom came and got me at the end of the gravel road

Bethybeth: cause it was really hot that day

Me: good. Sorry that happened, though.

Bethybeth: yea

Bethybeth: ttyl *(talk to you later)*

Bethybeth: leanne needs the computer

Although I believe that some of Beth's conversations were intended to elicit my shock and, in some cases, sympathy, I feel that she saw me as a "safe" voice in a "safe" space with whom she could privately commiserate and share feelings of frustration. As in the conversation between Aza and Ally, Beth demonstrated her power over her life by using IM not only to report her anger with her mother to another person (in some ways, the ultimate way to rebel against a parent) but also to demonstrate to me that she was tough enough to show her anger by doing what she characterized as running away from home. In this way, she not only empowered herself through the use of IM and choice of disclosure, but also constructed herself as powerful through her language and narrative.

IM: A New Interactive Diary

In her book *The body project: An intimate history of American girls* (1997), historian Brumberg used adolescent girls' diaries taken from different eras from the late 1880s through the late 1990s for historical evidence of girls' feelings about their bodies and sexuality. She wrote that "diaries reveal so much about the heart of being a girl" and "adolescent diaries persist, providing generations of girls with a way to express and explore their lives and feelings" (Brumberg, 1997, p. xxvii). Of the historical and cultural value of girls' diaries, Brumberg wrote,

> Old diaries are a national treasure, providing a window into the day-to-day routines of family, school, and community. They also recapture the familiar cadences of adolescent emotional life, and they provide authentic testimony to what girls in the past considered noteworthy, amusing, and sad, and what they could or would not talk about. (p. xxvii)

None of the girls interviewed for this book said they kept a print diary or journal, but one of them, Jordan, said she soon hoped to launch her own Xanga, the blog referred to in one of her previous conversations, which is an online equivalent of a diary that is meant for public display. Although her blog was somewhat unusual at the time that I first gathered the data and conducted interviews for this book, it has become far more popular for adolescents to record their daily lives in blogs (Fillion, 2005; Kornblum, 2005); in fact, one study that surveyed blogs found that 58 percent of them were kept by adolescents aged thirteen to nineteen (Perseus, 2005, http://www.perseus.com/blogsurvey/geyser.html). Adolescents use blogs, which are often housed on social networking sites like Bolt.com and MySpace.com,[10] to express the personal details of their lives in narrative form and to express their preferences (e.g., television shows, music, and fashions). More often than not, they give the URL and permission to read their blogs only to friends and people with whom they are familiar—often constituting an audience of only a dozen or so (MacDonald, 2005). Some blogs are password protected to ensure an exclusive audience, and others are available to anyone who happens upon them. However, most blogs are published in such a way that only the primary author of the blog may post to it; there are exceptions that allow readers to respond both publicly (at the bottom or to the side of the blog's main posting space) and privately (through email or a screen that can be read only by the blog's author), though most blogs are a one-to-many communication with little chance for immediate interactivity. Blogs are online diaries and journals and very much in the same vein of what Brumberg wrote about in her research on adolescent girls' diaries; they are the twenty-first century's most obvious version of the diary.

In the discussion of IM serving as a private space, it is interesting to question whether it may also function as a diary, particularly because so many of the girls interviewed for the book said they often saved and stored past conversations on their hard drives or printed the conversations and stored them in the privacy of their bedrooms. Some characterized their saved and printed conversations as "important" or especially "funny" conversations, and they kept them in order to look back and review those conversations in the future.

"I just sometimes like to remember what we talked about," Beth said, "but sometimes I want to keep it because it's funny." In this sense, IM conversations function similar to a diary—although thoughts are articulated through interactivity with others rather than through introspection.

"I like to look back and remember what I was talking about with people and what I was saying," Lindsay said in her interview. Although she said she sometimes does this in order to make sure that certain words and actions are a matter of record, she said she generally hopes to look back on the conversations and gain better understanding of what was going on in her social life at a certain point in time. Aza agreed, saying she liked to look back on the funnier conversations; however, she admitted she had just saved a few fights that had occurred on IM with a recent ex-boyfriend that led to a painful breakup. Her friend Nicole went to even greater lengths to save conversations by utilizing what she referred to as "dead IM," or a tool within IM that makes it appear as if a user is always online (though when they are not using the IM for more than fifteen minutes, their log-in name in the window becomes gray instead of the usual black); however, this feature also triggers a "log manager," which automatically saves all conversations within a temporary file folder on the computer. She said she occasionally read through her old IM logs "just for fun," though she worried about her mother discovering them.

In this regard, communication through IM may be emerging as a primary source for how some adolescents conceive of themselves and take on an identity. This is significant because within traditional diaries, girls' discussion of personal events include commentary on particular feelings associated with those events (e.g., how a girl feels about her first period), but within IM, little personal reflection is apparent. Instead thoughts are negotiated through conversation with another person or persons, and expression of feelings is not private but interactive.

Furthermore, this demonstrates a major cultural shift. Brumberg asserts that girls in the late nineteenth and early twentieth centuries did not write about topics that they considered extremely personal (e.g., first periods and intimacies with young men) in their diaries because, she surmises, the topics felt embarrassing to the girls even within a locked book. Moreover, broaching such topics was not culturally acceptable (Brumberg, 1997). However, over the years, girls slowly disclosed more and more personal details within their diaries until, by the 1980s, they disclosed not only feelings about their changing bodies but also very graphic accounts of heterosexual and lesbian sexual encounters (Brumberg, 1997). Now, in the new millennium, it seems girls disclose relatively sensitive information in ways that could be construed as very public. For example, in the online bulletin boards on gURL.com (Grisso & Weiss, 2005), girls candidly and explicitly discuss with one another topics ranging from how to give a blowjob to whether it is fine to have premarital sex. The IM conversations that the girls in this book provided often disclosed personal details about their bodies and their sexual identities, and much like in the online bulletin boards, they discussed these details with others and saved the conversations. Unlike with the online bulletin boards, which are made up of anonymous strangers posting with log-in names, the conversations were personal disclosures hashed out among friends and acquaintances, and the conclusions were shared with each other.

The historical diaries studied by Brumberg contained thoughts so private that the girls felt they could not be shared; they were never meant to be consumed by the public and even when Brumberg did use them as data for her book, the stories were completely anonymous—even Brumberg did not know to whom the diaries belonged. However, in a culture that has made reality television programs some of the most watched among all demographic groups, negotiation of identity in the public eye (within the public discourse) is not only entertaining but also seemingly honorable to many. It is notable that this particular form of entertainment was first launched by a network that has always been extremely popular with adolescents, MTV (MTV's "Real World" debuted in 1992 but reality shows still fill the bulk of the hours of programming on the channel) (www.MTV.com, 2006). As the viewership for reality television shows increases among younger generations and as larger portions of the population apply to be on them, the acceptance of public identity negotiation (through reality television and other media, such as IM and blogs) could broaden dominant cultural discourses. In fact, this new generation's increased value placed on surveillance has already arguably proved to be economically lucrative for corporations that expect audiences to continue to value watching real people on TV because their advertising revenues have more than paid for the cheap programming (Andrejevic, 2003). If public surveillance and performance continue to be valued so highly, both economically and culturally, it stands to reason that people will become less apt to engage in private, internal identity negotiation and more inclined to air their shifting personal feelings in public. Broadcasting personal feelings and identity shifts may become the cultural norm, and the idea of safe, private space may no longer be relevant.

This could be particularly true of adolescents. Adolescents—some of the heaviest users of IM and all of whom grew up in a generation that is comfortable with technology—simply may be accustomed to interactive exchanges of ideas, even when the ideas involve the personal details of their lives. Adolescent girls especially value online communication as a means to develop and extend relationships that they already have in their lives (Clark, 2005). As you can see through the conversations that the girls submitted for this book, IM allows for adolescent girls to mull over personal subject matter with peers, and, in many cases, the girls know that they are not necessarily alone in feeling uncomfortable about certain events and feelings about their lives. For example, Sunny said that she saved the following conversation because it was important to her. Clearly, it represents a negotiation between her spirituality and sexuality, and these feelings are validated by a friend she met at Bible camp who struggled with the same emotions. Moreover, she said that she would not share these feelings with friends from school; the friend from Bible camp (who lives in another city) has no contact with most of her friends at school and therefore is a "safe" or private outlet for personal conversations.

Firekiss23: I MISS YOU!!!
Firekiss23: i miss (Bible) camp already
Nora: yea...
Nora: but stay on with Christ
Firekiss23: yes i know
Firekiss23: but sometimes, its soooo hard...
Nora: i feel ya pain yo
Firekiss23: like there's too many temptations

Firekiss23: u kno, like may gurls like marissa were saying that u inspired them.

Firekiss23: marissa says thanks

Nora: haha is not me it was God all him

In reading the conversation, Sunny takes on a somewhat different tone with this friend than she uses in other conversations with friends and boyfriends— a far less playful, more inquisitive tone that is at odds with the fun, flirty image she seems to project in other conversations and somewhat at odds with the physical image she presents (Sunny, whose log-in his Firekiss23, wears provocative clothing and a great deal of makeup in person). In talking with Nora on IM, she went further and actually asked specific, direct questions relating to spirituality. This is a very different conversation from the other conversations she submitted, in which she seems very sure of herself and very willing to explore sexuality and adulthood in many ways.

Firekiss23: i just dunno how to deal with tempatations. do u just pray?

Nora: well do this from now on.

Nora: wenever yoo wanna do something bad

Nora: juss think of me and God

Nora: ^_^

Firekiss23: oh yea i should do that...

Firekiss23: i just hope that i can have strong faith like u

Nora: well if you want a faith like me

Nora: yoo need to give up

Nora: your all to God

Nora: i gave up make up and hair styles

Nora: yoo saw the way i look now hahah

Firekiss23: but u still look pretty

Firekiss23: serouisly

Firekiss23: * seriously

Nora: hahahahaha

Nora: thanx your so adorable

Firekiss23: haha thanx...

Firekiss23: but those are hard to give up, ya kno

In the last two lines, Sunny seemed to acknowledge that she enjoyed the part of her identity relating to her fashion and style choices but seemed to imply that she might be willing to give up this part of her lifestyle if it better fit the "Christian" identity that she also appears to value. She went on:

Nora: trust me
Nora: I WAS BOY CRAZY
Nora: WEN I WAS ONLY IN 678 GRADE
Firekiss23: O....
Nora: hahahah bit i realize why do i want to impress them
Nora: there juss perverted and likes to touch people
Firekiss23: oh yea
Firekiss23: they're all jerks
Nora: and its not like they would die for me
Firekiss23: yeah that's totally true
Nora: yea... but God will never break your heart
Firekiss23: yea exactly
Nora: andyoo know wen yoo go to school
Nora: its REALLY GONNA BE HARD
Nora: God should always be number one priority
Firekiss23: ic ic...

As will be seen from other conversations between Sunny and friends from school, this conversation is *not* a strong representation of what Gee refers to as her "situated identity" (Gee, 1999, p. 36), or the characteristic way of "coordinating or getting coordinated by other people, things, tools, technologies, symbol systems, places, and times" (Gee, 1999, p. 36)—at least with regard to the characteristic way that she presents herself in interviews and all of her other conversations submitted for this book. In the interviews and IM conversations with classmates that you will read in Chapter Four, Sunny generally paints herself as happy go lucky, flirty, and shopping-crazy. Rather, this conversation takes into account a shifting of identity—an attempt to understand and articulate herself in a spiritual way that calls into question her characteristic modes of behavior (wearing makeup and sexy clothing, flirting with boys). Again, it is notable that this is a conversation that she chose to save (and chose to submit to me, a researcher and a stranger—a topic that will be explored further in Chapter Six) and read again in the future because it demonstrates how identity (both gender and religious identity) can be enacted in the guise of an "interactive" journal.

What Does It Mean When a Diary Isn't Just Your Own?

Although Sunny is the participant in the previous conversation who actually gave permission for me to use a very personal conversation about her religious and sexual identity, Nora—a girl whom I never met and who did not participate in any of the other conversations that Sunny submitted to me—was the girl doing most of the talking in the conversation and disclosing much of her personal information.[11] In fact, the contents of the conversation actually represent far more overt discussion of identity negotiation on Nora's behalf, particularly in her disclosures of how she used to be "boy crazy" and obsessed with how she looked but had "given it all up" because she felt it made her a better Christian. Because Nora was not a part of the study and remained anonymous to me, I was not able to ask her how she felt about Sunny keeping the conversation to serve as her own personal diary entry. (Sunny presumably let her know that she might pass it along for the book's research.) This again suggests that girls seem to value their ability to use the new media technology to manage their social lives (and in this case, private lives) so much so that trust must be assumed and negotiated within each message (Clark, 2005). As Clark suggests, this type of online disclosure represents "wider, geographically located social networks that are characterized by immediate, possibly intimate connections with others and that vary in intensity not by one's association with a particular social substructure or even a particular social group," but instead by a "much more individually organized social network, one that is organized around concerns about how one is able to present oneself in relation to what one perceives as the desired image for different peers" (Clark, 2005, p. 217).

The implications of this importance placed on presentation of self are enormous when thinking about IM as a personal diary. The idea suggests that even though Sunny and others might consider the conversations they keep as important reminders of their past and on-the-record negotiations with issues in their daily lives, the diary itself could vary wildly based on the response of the other person chatting. Had Nora told Sunny that it was fine to be crazy, Sunny might have responded far differently than to admit that her sexual temptation felt un-Christian. Although the IM conversations that the girls save are iteratively constructed, they are indeed merely just constructions (or reconstructions, considering that they must rely on memory to place the conversation into the historical context in which it took place). The conversations that are used, arguably, as a substitute for a traditional diary equipped with a lock and key, are still a valued artifact that the girls choose to represent their pasts, but these artifacts are very different from the bound paper diaries of years past. This practice does beg the question of how the difference of a peer-to-peer construction of life events and personal thoughts used as a diary may affect the very nature of the *use* of a diary—to record memories, to sort through private thoughts, to articulate personal values. When considering how a traditional diary may be used to negotiate personal feelings and attitudes and even to cultivate attitudes that may extend into adulthood, it is important to question whether an interactive type of diary can serve the same function. After all, identity in this regard might be constructed based on the whims of a conversational partner in an exchange that is rapid and ephemeral, rather than on careful internal contemplation.

Keeping in mind that IM functions as a private space where identity may be interactively negotiated, I will continue to explore cultural narratives that became apparent through the girls' IM conversations in the next chapter. This analysis hones in on a dominant recurring narrative in their conversations: how gender identity—and especially gender identity associated with sexuality—is constructed and negotiated through IM.

CHAPTER FOUR
"LOL—im gonna make out w/ so many ppl tomrw~": Negotiating Gender Identity through IM

Adolescence is biologically and culturally a time when individuals undergo sexual development and begin to incorporate interpretations of what it means to be "sexy" within the context of mass-mediated culture. Furthermore, notions of what culture constitutes as feminine (and often sexy) are often solidified during adolescence, a time when girls surround themselves with magazines, television shows, popular films, and consumer products that all peddle a normative femininity and sexuality that girls often believe can be both purchased and emulated. In adolescence, girls oftentimes perform gender based on the mass media's images of what they feel an adolescent girl is supposed to be—even if it's impossibly tough and sexy like Buffy the Vampire Slayer or Veronica Mars or vacant and impossibly thin like many of the models and celebrities staring at them from the pages of *ELLEGirl* and *Teen People*. The images of adolescent girls in the media are often rather unrealistic portrayals of gender that can make such performances difficult and unhealthy.

But even though adolescent girls are at a relatively turbulent developmental period as they navigate through mass culture's construction of girls and femininity, it does not mean that they buy into the dominant cultural ideal of the perfect adolescent girl. And one might believe that through the Internet—a medium that allows anyone to publish what they wish through blogs and Web pages, and mandates that people communicate without the benefit (or hindrance) of face-to-face communication— adolescent girls may resist the unrealistic images of young women perpetuated by the media. IM in particular presents a new opportunity for adolescent girls to more easily "say" what they are thinking and assert themselves in ways that defy dominant cultural notions of girlishness; because of its mass adoption by adolescent girls and their perception that it is easier to say something over IM than in person or over the phone (Clark, 2005; Lewis & Fabos, 2000; Thiel, 2005), it would seem like the perfect cultural moment for girls to say what they like online to each other and to the world. As cultural producers through this new media (Mazzarella, 2005), girls would seem to be in a position to resist mass culture's constructions of femininity, girlhood, and sexuality.

However, despite the opportunity to resist these stereotypical constructions, and despite the fact that girls tend to break the mold of girlishness with other girls (as was demonstrated with their very direct verbal arguments presented in the previous chapters), the girls who participated in the research for this book lapsed into dominant gender norms associated with teenage girls. Many of the IM conversations included flirtatious conversations between girls and boys—sometimes with boyfriends and sometimes simply boys from school whom they hardly knew. In many cases, the language they used was very sexually explicit and often the girls made rather overt sexual references (whether this is an act of empowerment or "just having fun" is a matter that differs among the girls). Other times, they were coy in their language and mannerisms simply hinting that they were "sexy"—or at least sexy online. Moreover, a number of the girls converse primarily online with their boyfriends, from discussing intimate secrets to simply making plans for dates, and some said these conversations have drawn them closer. In many of these conversations, it became apparent that traditional gender roles were being played out, such as that of a caretaker/mother. This chapter analyzes how these varied understandings of sexuality and gender roles are apparent through IM.

Sexuality: Experimentation and Empowerment
In reading through the girls' conversations, it becomes apparent that adolescent girls on IM appear to experiment with notions of sexuality and relational dynamics with members of the opposite sex. (None of the girls in the study identified themselves as gay.) In viewing this idea as a cultural model, IM becomes a space in which its users are able to negotiate and understand sexuality without having to rely upon bodies. Sexuality among adolescents may be played out in various ways online (Clark, 1998; Grisso & Weiss, 2005; Stern, 2001), and in IM, this is done not only within the conversational narratives, but also through the use of log-in names and profiles.[12] When using AIM or Yahoo Instant Messaging services, users may only register for one log-in name at a time, and that name is the one that appears within girls' conversations until they decide to open a new accountwith a different log-in name. Often, these log-in names play with their given names or nicknames and involve favorite numbers. However, the girls who used MSN Instant Messaging had the ability to change their user

name as often as they liked and often did so once or twice per week (AOL and Yahoo! users do not have this capability). In the case of MSN log-in names, girls often opted for song lyrics or well-known clichés that described their feelings at a given moment, or they came up with phrases referencing private jokes between themselves and their friends. Although the girls' log-in names cannot be reproduced here in the interest of their privacy, the names and phrases often ascribed some kind of identity to the person (whether true or false). For example, thirteen-year-old Leanne, who changed her log-in names frequently, used "Leanne is SEXY!!!" as a log-in name for a period of time, and fifteen-year-old Aza used a sexually explicit line from a rap song as her log-in for a few weeks. Furthermore, within their online profiles (discussed in an earlier section), girls sometimes described themselves in terms that expressed sexual desire. For example, in the IM fight between Nicole and her friend over content within the friend's profile, there were references to Nicole as a "slut" while the friend bragged about being "close" (sexually) to Nicole's boyfriend.

Most often, the online exchanges about sexuality were playful and, if with members of the opposite sex, flirty. The point that adolescent girls feel comfortable and positive about expressing sexuality is very important; girls in decades past tended to feel embarrassed about expressing sexuality outside the pages of their private diaries (and even within them) and with using sexual overtones in conversations with members of the opposite sex (Brumberg, 1997). Girls in my research on IM might appear to transgress the social norms associated with "nice" girls in the past (Brown & Gilligan, 1992; Finders, 1996), even if they approach sexuality with a certain degree of playfulness and coyness. A conversation between Sunny and a male friend exemplifies this:

> **Firekiss23:** tomm's national kissing day! Lol
> **Firekiss23:** so that means u and me gotta kiss
> **SlimmXx44:** lol suuuuuuuuure ;-)
> **SlimmXx44:** ok fine
> **SlimmXx44:** what about jenni?
> **Firekiss23:** i thought u liked ariel
> **SlimmXx44:** wtf *(what the fuck)*
> **Firekiss23:** do u think she's cute?
> **SlimmXx44:** do u

Firekiss23: how would i kno? im a gurl
SlimmXx44: i wanna kiss u
Firekiss23: lol stop playin
SlimmXx44: Sunny i do
Firekiss23: lol im gonna make out w/ so many ppl *(people)* tomrw~
SlimmXx44: k me and u ok
Firekiss23: OK lol

Sunny is the same girl in the previous chapter who had a very serious conversation with a friend from Bible camp about being tempted by sex. The previous conversation about "making out with so many people" on National Kissing Day took place within the same month, which really demonstrates how an adolescent girl can manipulate tone and negotiate the many disparate discourses surrounding her in a relatively short time period. This is consistent with the literature that sees the Internet as a space where identities can be constructed, cast off, and reconstructed (Rheingold, 1993; Turkle, 1995), and somewhat defies adolescents' own assertion that they express a more truthful sense of self online than they do in other aspects of their lives (Clark, 1998; Tobin, 1998). However, it also reaffirms Hall's point (1996) that identity is never fixed but shifts constantly as people locate themselves within the cultures in which they live. In this way, it is easy to see how Sunny could be a forthright churchgoer in one IM conversation and a sexy flirt in another.

In the following conversation, Sunny uses the same flirtatious tone with a boy she has been seeing and, in the same seemingly lackadaisical manner, discusses "making out" with another boy:

THEEDUDE7: when did he feeeeeeel your skin??? Hahaha
Firekiss23: lol well not really .. i made out with him ~ lol
THEEDUDE7: ooo ic ic.
Firekiss23: hehe during lunch
THEEDUDE7: today?
Firekiss23: no Friday
Firekiss23: lol theres this place where ppl *(people)* make out. we went there and no one was there.
Firekiss23: hehehe
Firekiss23: yea but don't tell anyone ~~
THEEDUDE7: i won't

THEEDUDE7: so
THEEDUDE7: is he a good kisser
Firekiss23: lol yea, i gess. i was first asain *(Asian)* for him, and he's first black to me
THEEDUDE7: oooooo
Firekiss23: yea ~ lol anywayz
THEEDUDE7: so do u like him
Firekiss23: idk *(I don't know)*. i think he's cute and nice but i like this other black guy, not him.
Firekiss23: well, it's not even "like" .. just think he's cuter than him. dont tell him.
Firekiss23: u know how im *(I am)*. i don't "like" ppl *(people)*. i just think they're cute
Firekiss23: yeah but i still think ur *(you are)* cute

Sunny's conversation with THEEDUDE7 then shifts from her playfully discussing sexuality. Within the conversation, we learn that she not only likes to articulate her identity within IM conversation as flirty and somewhat experienced with making out with boys, but she also places particular emphasis on race simply by noting it. (He was the first African American she had kissed whereas she was the first Asian American he had kissed. She actually "likes" another African American whose race she also notes.) She continued to articulate and negotiate a sexual identity as she interactively conversed with the guy friend, who it becomes apparent she had been dating in some capacity, and in the next part of the conversation we can see how she (somewhat flippantly) breaks off her romantic relationship with him.

Firekiss23: how bout u? how's ur luv life? u don' t like me no more, rite?
Firekiss23: u kno, we've been "together" and now, i think its over..
Firekiss23: dats wat u think, too, rite
THEEDUDE7: well i still care about you but since we cant like be "together" anymore yeah
THEEDUDE7: dang when was the first time i met u
Firekiss23: like 1.5 months ago?
Firekiss23: we've been together for like a month
THEEDUDE7: dang
THEEDUDE7: thats long time
Firekiss23: but i think we can be good friends ~ like really good friends. do u wanna?
THEEDUDE7: yeah
Firekiss23: cuz ur really cool and i don't wanna just let u go ~ lol idk *(laugh out loud—I don't know)*

As the conversation with THEEDUDE7 continues, Sunny articulates her feeling that she might be appearing lackadaisical because she has been hurt in previous relationships with boys. In this section, she demonstrates a less flirty, more introspective (and very much adult) tone. However, in the last line she returns to her flirty, seemingly appearance-conscious persona.

> **Firekiss23:** like i said i still care about you but we cant be together anymore
> **THEEDUDE7:** yea same here
> **THEEDUDE7:** but the only thing is that i just dont want u to get hurt by guys which i dont think will happen to u
> **Firekiss23:** omg *(oh my God)* ur *(you are)* understanding this too well.. ur soo cool. thank you
> **THEEDUDE7:** seriously
> **Firekiss23:** i've gotten hurt by guys in the past so i don't want that anymore
> **Firekiss23:** maybe dat's why im like this now.
> **THEEDUDE7:** ciz ive seen on tv and all that shit about girls who like get depressed and hurt themselves cuz they cant find a guy to like love and shit
> **Firekiss23:** oh
> **THEEDUDE7:** u mean like guys in korea or here
> **Firekiss23:** here
> **THEEDUDE7:** like who tony
> **Firekiss23:** lol nope. i didn't care about him. i just liked the way he looked.

The girls also appeared comfortable with discussing sexual matters with their female friends. Upset from an IM conversation with her recent ex-boyfriend about his own sexual experience, Jordan ("starchicachic") wonders whether she should ask if he was still a virgin. However, she said in her interview that she would never ask such a personal question of him in person:

> **starchicachic:** i can't decide whether to ask him if he is still a virgin
> **Michele:** do
> **Michele:** then tell me
> **starchicachic:** i don't think i will
> **starchicachic:** i'm afraid of the answer

Later in the conversation, though, Jordan and her friend take on more playful tones in discussing sexuality and sex education. This part of the conversation may be slightly less shocking in the context of two seventh-grade girls discussing sexuality and also more commonplace in the discussion of sexuality among the girls in this book:

Michele: im in sex ed and mr waggner asked us 1. wats sex

Michele: 2. wats oral sex

starchicachic: ack

starchicachic: fun

starchicachic: thats ok

starchicachic: my hot science teacher gives us sex ed whenever he feels like it

Michele: and jake answered "sex in when a guy stiks his penis into somes vagina, and oral sex is when a man stiks his penis into a girl moth or his tonge into her vagina"

Michele: im sorry

starchicachic: ack

In these and other IM conversations, the discussion of sexuality greatly differs from girl to girl with regard to how explicitly she speaks about it, but each of the girls appeared to be comfortable with the discussion, regardless of her race and geographic location. In the IM conversations outlined above, the girls defied typical traditional notions of girls as shy and innocent as each of them demonstrated progressive views about sexuality (e.g., Jordan's concern over her ex-boyfriend's sexual exploits and desire to ask him about whether he has lost his virginity, and Sunny casually breaking up with a boy and asking to be friends while telling him about making out with new boyfriends). This seemingly new progressive—and often aggressive—sexuality has been explored in recent literature about adolescent girls and offline identity (Lamb, 2001; Simmons, 2002) as well as in Grisso and Weiss's (2005) chapter about adolescent girls who write about sex and sexual topics in the online bulletin boards on the gURL.com, a Web site for girls aged thirteen and older, and is currently owned by dELia*s Corp., a clothing retailer (Grisso & Weiss, 2005). In the online forums, girls ask other girls questions about definitions related to sexuality (e.g., "what is a blo job?"; p. 35) or for advice regarding actually having and enjoying sex (e.g., "…When my bf and I r h avingv sex and I'm on top I don't think he enjoys it as much. Wat can I do to make him like it more?" (p. 42). The authors note that in the process of conversing online, both the girls asking and answering the questions tend to construct and perform identities that would make the other participants in the online conversation realize that they are either sexually experienced or sexually naïve. Although the girls who participate in the gURL.com bulletin boards are anonymous to one another (they use log-in names that give little personal information), they tend to form a community that is somewhat like the girls who speak with one another on IM. A high level of trust is apparent in the online bulletin boards of gURL.com, and (especially considering the possibility that their conversations on IM will be cut and paste into other conversations passed along by their peers) a high level of trust is also apparent in IM conversations.

Girls' increased awareness of sexuality, including an increased willingness to discuss it publicly and acknowledge sex as a part of their lives in IM and in online forums may suggest not only a healthy knowledge of sexuality and the body that has not always been present in the lives of adolescent girls, but also a willingness to better understand the physical and emotional ramifications of sex. However, the next section will explore how negotiation of sexual identity online is often tied into the performance of feminine gender (as a binary opposite to masculine gender), and how patriarchal discourses displace healthy conversation about sexuality between girls and boys.

Sexuality and Dominant Cultural Discourses

Although, through IM, the girls in this study appeared to feel more comfortable with confrontation and frank discussion of sexuality and other topics as well as free to flout linguistic norms, the narratives of their IM conversations were often mired in the dominant cultural discourses that cater to male desire and power. Just as their log-in names and profiles often suggested strong articulation of sexual identity, they also reflected strong leanings toward perceived norms of femininity and domesticity. For example, Leanne (though she just turned thirteen while taking part in this research) used "I really, really, really need a boyfriend!!!" for several weeks as her log-in name after giving up her previous one, "Leanne is SEXY!!!" In an IM conversation submitted by Nicole, her female friend, Alysa, referenced a quote from a movie that Nicole then planned to put into her profile:

> **Alysa:** *Most of all I'm scared of walking out of this room and never feeling again the way I feel when I'm with you*
> **junkytrunk:** :-/ :-/'

Alysa: aint that cute
junkytrunk: yes it is
junkytrunk: who said dat
Alysa: its a quote
Alysa: jana sent it to me
junkytrunk: im boutta put dat in my profile
junkytrunk: im puttin it in
Alysa: okay

The movie quote that neither girl could place appeared in the teen dancing film, *Dirty Dancing* with Jennifer Grey and Patrick Swayze, which was released in 1987 (before many of the girls who participated in this study were born). However, the small piece of popular culture that Nicole plans to borrow for her profile demonstrates not only the pervasiveness of popular culture (especially now that it is so easy to reproduce memorable movie quotations on the Internet) but also the pervasiveness of romantic storylines from films. In this particular line, Jennifer Grey has told Patrick Swayze, essentially, that she does not want to leave him because he completes her. Even without the film's storyline to back it up, Nicole finds the idea of the quotation so compelling and romantic that she would like to use it to represent her IM profile.

Often, discussions of sexuality are playful among girls talking to one another on IM, with topics ranging from breast size to comments about "hot guys," and sometimes they are frank as in the conversations relayed in the previous chapter with girls discussing sex in the context of religion and in the context of biology class. However, in the IM conversations between girls and boys, dominant patriarchal discourses that position girls as the weaker, nicer sex are often apparent, even when the conversations are meant to be playful. Much of the cultural discourse surrounding adolescents centers on the importance that adolescents attach to sexiness and sexuality (Durham, 2001), and judging by the conversations submitted by the girls in this research, IM—even though it is a disembodied medium—does not appear to be a space that is free from this discourse. For example, in separate conversations between girls and boys that were submitted by fifteen-year-old Aza, thirteen-year-old Jordan, fourteen-year-old Beth, and fifteen-year-old Caitlyn, the boys jokingly referred to the girls participating in sexualized lesbian acts. Jordan pasted an excerpt of a conversation she was having with a male friend from school at the same time that she conversed with her best friend, Liz, whose log-in name is kindYlizzee, on how a play on the word "bye" so easily lead to joking about bisexuality.

> **starchicachic:** u should not have said bi
> **starchicachic:** they think that we had "hot lesbian sex" now
> **kindYlizzee:** kewl *(Jordan pastes other conversation)*
> > **9Josh7:** shes bi?
> > **9Josh7:** its that your girlfirned jordan?
> > **9Josh7:** did you guys have hot lesbian sex?
> > **9Josh7:** i feel loved
> **starchicachic:** damn
> **kindYlizzee:** o! ic
> **kindYlizzee:** sry jordan!
> **starchicachic:** i hate u guys so mcuh
> **kindYlizzee:** ha

In some ways it is surprising (and perhaps a little bit heartening in a way) that an alternative discourse to the dominant heterosexual norm is apparent in the conversations; after all, adolescents are so rarely offered alternative discourses within mainstream media and culture. The notion that heterosexuality is "normal" is also seen in the gURL.com online forums described by Grisso and Weiss (2005), particularly in the phrase, "UR A LESBO!" in response to a girl's question about feeling attracted to other girls (p. 38). However, other girls in the online forum appear to be more accepting of bisexuality ("even if your suddenly bi, just go with it. it's the best of both worlds.") (p. 38). However, the particular references to lesbians and bisexual individuals in the IM conversations—which, unlike the gURL.com forum, often include boys—tend to reflect a male fantasy of women with women that is sexualized and unrealistically depicted in pornographic films, and the discourse is ultimately negative and patriarchal, as seen in this example of Caitlyn's boyfriend joking about the subject:

> **CaitlynKay:** aaron peters thinks me and marianne are lesbians
> **Nikeyguy1:** lol
> **Nikeyguy1:** sweet
> **Nikeyguy1:** haha
> **Nikeyguy1:** that would be cool

CaitlynKay: o no it wouldn't
Nikeyguy1: maybe it would be if u guys were bi
Nikeyguy1: lol
CaitlynKay: no no no
CaitlynKay: thats nasty
Nikeyguy1: not for me
CaitlynKay: boys are naasty

Grisso and Weiss (2005) point out that even in online environments where girls are speaking only with other girls, they are "limited in their ability to transcend the language and symbols of males" (p. 45), by telling their own narratives of sexuality using the linguistic norms and terms that are found in pornography geared toward men. Additionally, even in the online space that is supposed to be "safe" for free discussion, any girl who shows "excessive agency" or tells too much about her sexuality and experience is often scolded by another member of the community or reminded that she must adhere to certain dominant notions of femininity if she wants to be accepted by society (p. 45).

The girls in this book did not admonish their peers for speaking freely about sexuality in IM in most cases, but instead, demonstrated disgust with boys for making references to sexuality, as was exemplified in the last conversation from Caitlyn when she declared "Boys are nasty!" and in an earlier conversation between Jordan and Michelle when Jordan responds to a comment about the definition of oral sex with "ack." Jordan also scolds her own friends for playing along with Josh's jokes about her and her friends being lesbians when she writes, "i hate u guys so much."

Even while breaking up nonchalantly with her boyfriend and recalling exploits with other boys in a conversation in the previous chapter, Sunny often "giggled" within the parlance of IM (e.g., "lol" and "hehe"). Sunny said in her interview that she felt the need to use these conversational hedges in order to seem less aggressive and to appear more demure in her conversations with boys: "If it's a girl, I can talk about anything if I am close with her, but if it's a boy, I keep things secretive." As we attempt to understand how girls negotiate and articulate gender identity online, it becomes apparent how reflective Sunny's quotation is of a larger tug between the ways in which girls play into the dominant patriarchal discourses that place them in positions of weakness and the ways they transgress these discourses (Currie, 1999). How girls locate their situated identities within these cultural models of IM becomes an important line of discussion.

Dominant cultural discourses relating to male desire are often played out in the discourses of IM conversations, such as this one between thirteen-year-old Jordan and an ex-boyfriend, Mark, which quickly dissolves from a chat about whether they are attending a classmate's bar mitzvah to a discussion of his online sexual exploits. In an online conversation with me after she sent me this conversation, Jordan said Mark had been sending her IMs that made her uncomfortable, and even though she saw him weekly in Sunday school, he never made comments in person that made her uncomfortable.

> **Mark:** i just had phone sex, ... it was wierd
> **starchicachic:** y do u tell me all this stuff?
> **Mark:** i tell, ALL of my friends thats stuff, at least almost all
> **starchicachic:** o
> **starchicachic:** well
> **starchicachic:** 1 q *(one question):* wit WHO?
> **Mark:** oh, two girls that live in (city), but i have a crush on one of them,
> **starchicachic:** with TWO?
> **Mark:** yeah:-)
> **starchicachic:** omg *(oh my god)* . do they kno u r *(know you are)* such a player?
> **Mark:** i'm not. i don't try to get girls to sleep with me...wtf
> **starchicachic:** wtf? *(what the fuck?)*
> **Mark:** what the fuck
> **starchicachic:** i don't kno wut to say
> **Mark:** its not like you don't have options
> **starchicachic:** wut should i say?
> **starchicachic:** no 1 else i kno has phone sex wit a) multiple girls, b) ANYBODY!!

Although Jordan appeared to be disturbed by the conversation (a fact that she confirms in an IM conversation with a girlfriend) and demonstrated difficulty in engaging in it, Mark seemed intent on shocking and upsetting her with his online sexual exploits. In an interview about the incident, she said she thought he might have been lying to hurt her (they had only broken up a few weeks earlier), but she was not sure.

In the next conversation, Sunny was approached via IM by an older popular boy from school, "MichaelT," with whom she had never spoken in person but who remarked about her "hot" appearance. Despite the fact that he did not know her at all (exemplified by his question about whether she is a sophomore), he asks her out:

MichaelT: o tight, what r you doin after school tomorrow
Firekiss23: um, i dunno
Firekiss23: prolly nothing
MichaelT: ii have like a 3 hour wait until I have fo my game, u wanna chill
Firekiss23: yeah, why not
MichaelT: so are you a soph?
Firekiss23: no i am a freshman
Firekiss23: do i look old?
MichaelT: yea cause your hot
MichaelT: and thats tight
Firekiss23: um, i m NOT hot
MichaelT: um you have no say in this, your hot
MichaelT: hah
Firekiss23: no one thinks i am hot . hehe :;/
MichaelT: um i am afraid they do.
MichaelT: my friends think you are, i am like yeh and thats the chick i want
Firekiss23: he he really? dat's cool –
MichaelT: yeh
Firekiss23: i m the chick u want?
MichaelT: yeh
MichaelT: deff *(definitely)*
Firekiss23: o .. ic ;-)
MichaelT: o tight, the wink i love it

Just like in the earlier conversation when she broke up with a boyfriend, Sunny, in this conversation, appeared to use conversational language that made her appear demure and at once somewhat sexy. For example, her use of "hehe," or the equivalent of giggling online, and smiley faces or winking smiley faces. The conversation continues as the boy asks her to make out with him:

MichaelT: so what kinda chill do you wanna do, talk or um...

Firekiss23: i dunnol. what do u wanna do?

MichaelT: i wanna do the um..

MichaelT: I mean make out

Firekiss23: oh, um.. I'd like to, but I don't just make out with anyone. I mean we aren't even going out... hehe

MichaelT: well we could

Firekiss23: yeah we could

MichaelT: so you wanna go out

Despite previous conversations with boys in which she was somewhat frank about her feelings, Sunny reacted to the boy's compliments with modesty and did not immediately discount making out with him (though she suggested getting to know one another better by the end of the conversation). Though IM clearly provides a space in which Sunny can articulate identity, it often seems in her conversations with boys that she articulates an identity wrapped up in looking and acting sexy. (Note that her conversation about spirituality and temptation was with another girl.)

Gee's (1999) suggested that identifying "cultural models," which can be defined as "tools of inquiry" within discourse that can help people to mediate between institutional meanings and personal, culturally situated meanings. He says this identification is important because people tend to articulate their identity through cultural models (p. 58). Cultural models are often expressed through an individual's interaction with others (Gee, 1999, p. 58), and this can work not only in person but also online, such as in her interactions over IM. Gee presented a list of questions to help identify cultural models (1999, pp. 78–79), in which one of the most crucial questions is "What sorts of texts, media, experiences, interactions, and/or institutions could have given rise to these cultural models?" Looking at Sunny's conversations with the boys in which she performs her gender in a highly feminine sexual way, it becomes difficult to discount numerous other conversations in which she discusses her envy of the look of certain scantily clad models in the advertisements of Abercrombie & Fitch (one of her favorite stores) and her desire to look a certain idealized (and often sexualized) way that seems prevalent in fashion magazines today. These IM conversations of girls will be further examined in the next section, which focuses on how ideal bodies and physical sexiness are still a concern to girls in the online world.

Defining Feminine Bodies and Fashion in Cyberspace

The desire for sexiness and physical perfection might seem somewhat out of place in IM, a space where girls seem to transgress gender norms in so many ways and more remarkable, a space where bodies are not present. However, a dominant narrative within the IM conversations of girls who participated in the research for this book concerned physical appearance and body weight.

In addition, some of the conversations specifically referred to culturally acceptable physical appearances with regard to fashion conventions and the purchase of consumer goods that would help them achieve a culturally acceptable physical appearance. In this conversation, Sunny, fifteen, discusses birthday gifts that she expects to receive from her mother, invoking the particular brand names of clothing that she prefers. It is also noteworthy that Sunny, who is Korean but has lived in a Midwestern college town for several years and has dual citizenship, discusses fashion partially in terms of racial identification ("Some Asians wear Abercrombie") with Bill, another Korean American. Her comments about race and fashion are in response to Bill joking that he would be called "white" for wearing certain labels that are deemed "preppy" in their peer group (which is largely Asian American but living within a predominantly white population in the Midwest):

BillMON: wat u getting for your bday?

Firekiss23: my mom's getting me some clothes from abercrobmie. and my sis is getting me some clothes, too. lol i dunno about other ppl. i told them not to get me anything

BillMON: haha Abercrombie

BillMON: i wonder how much money u spent there in yoru life

Firekiss23: nah. im not that rich. unlike who~ lol

BillMON: hmmmm

Firekiss23: i just buy sale items.

BillMON: unlike joe?

Firekiss23: hehe YOU!!!

BillMON: haha whatever

BillMON: ive seen your clothes and stuff

BillMON: abercrombie like 905 dollars a shirt

Firekiss23: 9.05 dollars?

Firekiss23: if they're on sale, it's like 15-20 dollars.

BillMON: i was jk *(just kidding)*

Firekiss23: hehehe K

Firekiss23: where do u buy ur clothes?

BillMON: flea market, wal mart, goodwill

BillMON: hahaha jp

The next portion of the conversation troubles the idea of articulation of racial identity and ethnicity. Sunny brings up the notion of acceptable definitions Bill's race and hers with regard to how each dresses. Again, this is significant considering that scholars of computer-mediated communication in the past saw the online realm as a space where race and ethnicity were somewhat irrelevant, and where distinctions of gender, racial, and ethnic identity articulation were somewhat blurred (Haraway, 1991; Reid, 1991; Turkle, 1995):

Firekiss23: icic *(do you buy)* abercrobmie too?

BillMON: nah

Firekiss23: is it too preppy?

BillMON: joe would start makin fun of me

Firekiss23: hehe why???

BillMON: hed start callin me white boy

Firekiss23: hehe white boy.

BillMON: all right

Firekiss23: yea but a lotta anzs *(Asians)* wear abercrombie.

BillMON: i was jo *(joking)*

BillMON: i know

Firekiss23: hehehe yea

In the conversation about wearing Abercrombie & Fitch, Sunny described the look as potentially too "preppy" for Bill, who jokingly characterized the brand as one that would be preferred by whites ("white boy") and therefore not for him. Sunny often appears to articulate the notion that fashion and styles that she associated with Causcasians are her preference. This articulation may even cover eye color (hers are dark brown, like most Koreans, but she has planned to purchase green contact lenses), as is noted in this other conversation with Bill that had taken place the previous week:

Firekiss23: hehe i ordered color lenses today!!

BillMON: so yur eues are gunna be red

Firekiss23: hehe nope

Firekiss23: green

BillMON: hahah

BillMON: tight

Firekiss23: yea! uu should get color lenses too!

BillMON: y

Firekiss23: cuz its cool ~~~

BillMON: i like my black eyes

Firekiss23: ok lol

In another conversation when Sunny again discusses fashion, style, and, in this particular case, acceptable body type, she pasted an icon of a buxom yet thin female Abercrombie & Fitch model next to her log-in name (it does not show up here), replacing an older icon of Santa Claus that she had placed next to her log-in name for the previous week. Doing so happened to fall within a discussion about girls with "weird" bodies (just before the start of this conversation, Sunny and Bill discussed a girl from school whose body seemed "flat" and "weird") and girls with "perfect" bodies, one of whom Sunny said was her sister.

Firekiss23: my sis's body is like perfect!!! Hehe

BillMON: oh

BillMON: i wanna see tat icon larger

Firekiss23: wat icon?

Firekiss23: santa claus?

BillMON: no

BillMON: aber *(referring to an Abercrombie advertisement with a sexy girl in short cut-offs and a small bikini top)*

Firekiss23: hehe do u like it

BillMON: no i thought it was u

Firekiss23: okay stop playin

Bill: hahaha

BillMON: ok now i know wat u look at in your spare time

Firekiss23: heheheh!!!

Firekiss23: i wish my body is like this

Firekiss23: no im not like that

BillMON: aight

BillMON: ive never seen your body like that so idk *(i don't know)*

Firekiss23: hehe no ones ever seen my bod like that cuz I don't do gross stuff
Firekiss23: lol

It is interesting to note that in her comment "I don't do gross stuff," Sunny equates a curvy body showing a lot of skin with actually being nude and having sex, which she suggests here that she does not do (though in previous conversations, she referenced "making out" with boys). Again, she presents herself in a particular way to this male friend that is very different from the way she presented herself to the older boy from school, Michael, who asked her to "chill out" with him after school, and it is still somewhat different than the identity she performed with her friend from Bible camp.

Furthermore, Sunny said, "I wish my body is like this," referring to the blonde model, who wore very short shorts, a cropped top, and appeared impossibly thin and yet large-breasted—bringing this online conversation very much into the offline world by referencing the sort of body that the mass media uses to advertise clothing. Conversations about weight and eating were prevalent among girls from all races and classes, a finding which somewhat opposes findings from studies in the 1990s that demonstrated African-American girls as having more positive body image than whites and little reason to discuss weight (Milkie, 1999; Orenstein, 1994). However, it is more consistent with recent studies that signal growingly negative body images associated with African-American girls (Ward, 2003). However, African-American girls' insecurities tended to focus on simply not having what they envisioned as an ideal body type, and this was tied closely to racial ideals of their gender. While some conversations referenced thinness as ideal (one of these is listed below), my interview data suggested that they actually did not always feel "thick" enough—or rather, somewhat larger and curvaceous— a consistency with recent cultural data on African-American adolescent girls' idealizing body image (Hesse-Beber, et. al., 2004). I had to ask for personal clarification on this point. For example, for a number of weeks, Aza used a screen name that said (something to the effect of) "my butt is fat." When asked about whether this was an insecurity, she said that actually, she wished her butt were larger and rounder and her waist thinner— something she identified as a cultural ideal among African-American girls in her peer group as is often exemplified by idealized women models and back-up dancers in hip-hop videos (Ward, 2003). The screen name was more in the realm of "wishful thinking," Aza said, but she did see "thick" as healthy and beautiful. She said she actually just felt that she was in general, "a little *too* thick" and "not curvy enough." This preoccupation with physical appearance is consistent with much of the research on adolescent girls and their internalization of media discourses about attaining the "perfect" body (Durham, 1996, 1999; McRobbie, 1982). The following is a typical conversation about body weight with Caitlyn, who is a healthy weight and athletic build, and her boyfriend, "Nikeyguy1," who is also white and fifteen:

CaitlynKay: can u believe i ran today
CaitlynKay: im proud
Nikeyguy1: wow
Nikeyguy1: where???
CaitlynKay: from whitts to the pool to the school then walked back cause we were dead
Nikeyguy1: cool
Nikeyguy1: i think i'll come over
CaitlynKay: ummmm
CaitlynKay: no stay and talk with me untli i go to sleep
Nikeyguy1: what if i want to talk to u face to face?
CaitlynKay: im sure u don't
CaitlynKay: and im like dead and still look like shit
Nikeyguy1: i bet u look good anyways
CaitlynKay: noooooo
CaitlynKay: i look fat
Nikeyguy1: bull shit
CaitlynKay: seriously
Nikeyguy1: if u look fat i look obese
CaitlynKay: i dont think so
Nikeyguy1: what ever

The following conversation takes place between Aza and a male classmate (also African American) whose log-in name is GoReDsKiNs! The conversation follows a discussion in which Aza urges Bryan to get a snack:

GoReDsKiNs!: FOOD!! im so fat!!!
Aza8: me too :-(
GoReDsKiNs!: are you?
Aza: yea :-(
GoReDsKiNs!: u know how much I weigh

Aza: lol

Aza: how much

GoReDsKiNs!: guess first

Aza: 167?

GoReDsKiNs!: nope

GoReDsKiNs!: lol

Aza: more or less?

GoReDsKiNs!: more

Aza: 190

GoReDsKiNs!: i aint that fat!

Aza: 185

GoReDsKiNs!: about 18..somethin

Aza: lol

GoReDsKiNs!: lol

GoReDsKiNs!: im fat for a skinny guy

Aza: no u aint

This conversation again represented a case in which Aza, who is a healthy weight and planning to audition for her school's step team, complained that she was too fat. However, this conversation represents an interesting phenomenon in that it served primarily to comfort *Bryan* about his body weight while Aza's weight was dropped from the conversation almost immediately. This conversation positioned Aza in the motherly role of caretaker or comforter, a role that manifests itself in a large number of the male–female IM conversations the girls submitted to me. This phenomenon will be explored in the following section.

Caretaking/Mothering Expressed through IM

With a few exceptions of demonstrations of friendship and unity, the girls described in my research appear to often antagonize, insult, and confront other girls on IM. However, it seems that they act much differently in conversations with boys, often offering comfort, advice, and reassurance to them via IM in ways that suggest they are comfortable in the role of caretaker. In the following conversation, Maggie, whose log-in is Number345, comforts a male classmate about a girl he has been seeing who recently started ignoring him:

SteveOh: i havent even talked to *(the girl he was seeing)* in 10 days

Number345: oic that sucks

SteveOh: things are prob. done with there

Number345: that sucks///

Number345: dammit shawn you need to take control

Number345: like call her or something

SteveOh: well now i dont even know if she likes me anymore

Number345: cause you dont call her

SteveOh: its too late to call like tomorrow

SteveOh: what if shes like "okay why is he calling me now"?

Number345: she wont be .. cause even if she doesnt like you like you then you are still friends

SteveOh: yeah, but i don't know

SteveOh: no one has even updated me with their conversations anymore ... like you or brenna

SteveOh: i feel like a loser now

Number345: what u mean

Number345: ?

SteveOh: you guys dont tell me anything about *(the girl)* anymore, and i dont see you now, i feel dumb

SteveOh: tell me what you heard lately

Number345: I DONT KNOW!!!

Number345: thats too open

Number345: narrow it down

SteveOh: like have you heard from her anything about me lately?

Number345: nope

Number345: sorry

SteveOh: all right ... damnit

The next conversation is between Caitlyn, who is Maggie's classmate, and her boyfriend, Luke, whose log-in name is Nikeyguy1. Luke has been drinking at the apartment of a friend's older sibling and begins IMing her from the apartment. Caitlyn drinks occasionally but was caught several weeks before this conversation and had been avoiding parties since as a result, even though it meant spending less time with her boyfriend. In this conversation, she attempts to talk him out of driving when he is drunk.

CaitlynKay: what did u do tonight?

CaitlynKay: or are u still doing?

Nikeyguy1: went to this apartment place

CaitlynKay: &?

Nikeyguy1: what do u mean??????

Nikeyguy1: ???????

CaitlynKay: i just member jared talkn about goin t a apartment and drinkin there

Nikeyguy1: when u talk to jared?

CaitlynKay: well i heard karla ask him why he was goin there

Nikeyguy1: where are u at right now

Nikeyguy1: scotts

Nikeyguy1: i think he went somewhere?

CaitlynKay: ic

Nikeyguy1: lol

Nikeyguy1: i am kinda lonely

CaitlynKay: so am i

Nikeyguy1: i am sorry

Nikeyguy1: where u at?

CaitlynKay: home

CaitlynKay: everyone is sleeping

CaitlynKay: *(her brother)* was asleep before i got home and i was home at 1030

Nikeyguy1: wow

Nikeyguy1: thats weird

Nikeyguy1: lol

CaitlynKay: shit im bored

Nikeyguy1: i think ii want to go drive around

Nikeyguy1: lol

CaitlynKay: noooooo

Nikeyguy1: i am good

CaitlynKay: noooooo

CaitlynKay: dont go

Nikeyguy1: i think i might stop by your house

Nikeyguy1: c u in 5 min

CaitlynKay: i think you shouldnt even drive

Nikeyguy1: i can drive

Nikeyguy1: i am fine

CaitlynKay: NO u cant

CaitlynKay: seriously don't

Nikeyguy1: lol!

CaitlynKay: i think u should stay

Nikeyguy1: why do u say that?

CaitlynKay: so u can talk to me

Nikeyguy1: i can drive out and talk to u

CaitlynKay: lol no thats ok i don't want u driving

Nikeyguy1: i aint that fucked up

CaitlynKay: still dont

All of these examples (and a number of similar others, which I did not include) point to girls taking on the role of caretaker with boys, whether the boys are friends or boyfriends. These examples demonstrate an ethic of care, the way in which a majority of girls and women attempt to solve problems in a way that cause the least disruption in relationships among people (Gilligan, 1982). This represents their "very strong sense of being responsible to the world" (Gilligan, 1982, p. 21), or in Tronto's view, represents a cultural burden (1993). In research studies conducted over girls' relationships in the 1990s, young girls in particular have been known to communicate with deference to members of the opposite sex and work for solutions by demonstrating that they care and are willing to work as problem-solvers (Brown & Gilligan, 1992; Pipher, 1994). In her landmark study, *In a different voice*, Gilligan (1982) wrote

> In the response to a request to describe themselves, all of the women describe a relationship, depicting their identity in the connection of future mother, present wife, adopted child, or past lover. Similarly, the standard of moral judgment that informs their assessment of self is a standard of relationship, an ethic of nurturance, responsibility, and care. (p. 159)

Gilligan, whose scholarship is based in psychology and was one of the first to study women, presents a framework for understanding women's identities that does not trouble the culturally constructed nature of gender, which is problematic in the context of this analysis. After all, gender is in large part a performance of how girls and women perceive their roles to be as they are understood within the culture in which they live (Butler, 1990).

One of the more dominant discourses is the notion that girls and women are caregivers—whether they are giving wives and mothers or caring daughters—and Tronto (1993) recognizes care as a gendered cultural ideal that is at the center of all humans' lives saying that it is not "a parochial concern of women, a type of secondary moral question, or the work of the least well off in society," but rather "a central concern of human life" that should be valued not only culturally but also politically and economically with regard to the fact that women—culturally constructed as the primary caregivers in most societies—are not paid or figured into the Gross National Product for caring for their children, husbands, and homes (Tronto, 1993, p. 180). Part of the devaluation of care comes from the idea that women are often assumed to be natural caregivers or are more altruistic (Folbre, 2001). Mothering is often culturally construed as natural and as a normalized identity for women (Ruddick, 1989, p. xi). Biologists discuss women's "natural" tendency to care for children as a product of their "investment" in mothering them since they carry children in their wombs and nourish them with breast milk as infants, but it is imperative to note that biological division of labor serves to keep patriarchal ruling classes in order (Folbre, 2001, p. 5) and women relegated to the margins of society.

Tronto (1993) suggests that there is always an assumption about caring being a burden upon the caregiver and distinguishes between caring for and caring about individuals or objects; specifically, she says, cultural expectation relates "caring for" to the needs of others whereas "caring about" is automatically equated to women caring for men (p. 349). The act and term become gendered in this meaning. In this argument, it imperative to note that care is not biological but rather culturally understood, and men can be taught to care and value care as much as women. According to Folbre (2001), this could easily happen if the economic ramifications of care were such that societies would lose money if men grasped motherly caregiving roles. However, discourses marking care as feminine are rampant in mediated texts (Durham, 1999; McRobbie, 1982) and perpetuated in modern culture. Most of the IM conversations submitted to me by the girls demonstrated care primarily with boys (as in the conversations listed above). In conversations among girls, when I expected to see an ethic of care expressed, the conversations generally were not as motherly or even friendly in tone. Often, they were somewhat distant and direct to the point of coldness, as is seen in this conversation between Michelle and Jordan, which took place after Jordan's conversation with ex-boyfriend Mark, about his online sex encounter:

starchicachic: mark is scaring me

Michele: sry *(sorry)*

starchicachic: no

Michele: u don't even kno

Michele: ignore him (thats wat im doing to hannah)

starchicachic: he just told me that he just finished having phone sex

Michele: tell him congradulations from me

starchicachic: omg *(oh my god)*

Michele: (no don't)

starchicachic: ur kidding me

Michele: sry

Michele: im tired

Michele: and i have low patients

starchicachic: lol

starchicachic: itz scar(r)ing

starchicachic: me

Michele: (and i think im comin down wit something)

starchicachic: :'(

starchicachic: ughish

starchicachic: do it just in time for hannas bm *(bat mitzvah)*

Michele: ill try

Michele: hey tell me if im comlplaing too much

starchicachic: ur not

starchicachic: don't worry

starchicachic: omg

Michele: wat

starchicachic: it wuz with 2 different girls!

Michele: tell him to go suk sum1s dik over the phone now

Michele: c wat he says

starchicachic: no

starchicachic: i asked if they knew he was a player

Michele: ok fine dont take my advice c what i care

starchicachic: lol

Although Jordan articulated how upset she was about Mark ("itz scar(r)ing me") up front, Michele joked about the situation and finally admitted that she was appearing to be less sympathetic to her problem because she was "tired," had "low patients" /*sic*/, and was "coming down with something." In response to Michele's admission that she was not feeling well, Jordan used an emoticon crying face [:'(], and then when Michele, seeming frustrated or else still joking wrote, "ok fine dont take my advice c what i care," Jordan responded with an "lol," signifying "laughing out loud," but really just seeming like a stock response as it often does among the IMers. Many of the conversations the girls submitted to me between them and other girls either demonstrated conflict, or just short, simple chatter— sometimes fun and sometimes rather trite and rife with emoticons and short abbreviations. However, more often than not, the conversations that the girls submitted that took place between them and other girls demonstrated the opposite of the ethic of care—vicious fighting among each other, which is exemplified in the IM conversations in Chapter Two.

Although it might be that the girls found their conversations with boys more interesting than their conversations with girls and therefore submitted more of them to me, by and large, this type of shorthand and lack of sympathy seemed to appear in the conversations that they did choose to submit. (A discussion of the significance of their self-selected IM conversations will follow in Chapter Six.)

A study of how this link carries into the Internet—a space once thought to be free from many traditional gendered discourses—is paramount to understanding how to change that discourse. The girls who were interviewed and who submitted conversations for the research in this book perform gender in disparate ways, including by expressing an "ethic of care" with members of the opposite sex, but this concept is directly at odds with most IM conversations presented earlier in this analysis, particularly the ones in which girls assert themselves and ask direct questions that might cause conflict or in which they show reckless regard for others' feelings. Again, the girls' use of IM at once shows how they transgress typical gender norms and yet also, far too often, give in to the dominant and often harmful ideals of what it means to be a girl.

Although these stereotypical images of the "ideal" adolescent girl come largely from cultural consumption of the traditional mass media (such as magazines and television), most of us have yet to realize how much they also have seeped into the online world through careful clever marketing and advertising techniques. Over the past decade, the Internet has become arguably a very commercial space, from the banner ads on news Web sites to eBay. As one of the most desirable demographics of consumers and the most avid users of Web technologies, the extent to which corporations target adolescent girls online is hardly surprising. The next chapter will examine some of these marketing and advertising techniques and discuss how these relate to the findings within the girls' IM conversations.

CHAPTER FIVE
Marketing to Youth: The Commodification of Identity in the New Media Landscape

This book has so far examined the girls' actual IM conversations with their peers—conversations enabling them to construct and affirm their gender identities in the process. In order to provide a complete picture of the role of IM in girls' lives, however, it is crucial to understand how corporate and advertising outlets have interceded in this relationship in order to further their own interests. After all, the technology would not be widely available for free if there were not some other economic incentive for the companies that provide it. While these companies—including AOL/Time Warner, Microsoft, and Yahoo—realize that IM is one of the best ways to reach the sometimes elusive marketing demographic of adolescents who marketers refer to as millennials or Generation Y, few admit to having much success at doing so. This does not mean that they are not working on it, however. Using both traditional and nontraditional routes of marketing and advertising, companies are doing all that they can to target and engage with the teens who use IM and other new media technologies. This chapter investigates several of these strategies for selling to teens and tweens, and it examines how these corporate strategies also work to pigeonhole girls as vapid consumers and empty vessels of popular culture. The final question is, however, "Are the girls buying it?"

ADDING ADVERTISING TO THE CONVERSATION
One of the first modes of advertisement within IM was traditional banner advertising—the placement of ads across the top or bottom of the Instant Messenger's buddy list window, which is used by AOL's AIM service. These ads, which feature a myriad of products that are not necessarily geared toward adolescents—including cars, movie stores, and in-house ads for AOL and its parent company's online products—often contain moving pictures and flashy gimmicks that users may click on, thereby opening the advertisement in a regular Web page format so that they can learn more about and often even purchase the product. This is a standard advertising practice in the online world that dates back to some of the earliest Web sites; advertisers may pay for the ad placement or on a pay-per-click basis. They often measure their success with banner advertising by measuring how many

people actually click on the ad and read the content afterward (this is called a "click-through" rate). As was the case with display advertising in newspapers and magazines, the effectiveness of banner ads has been questioned, but few other alternatives for revenue have been developed in the years since the Web became a desirable commercial space (Smith, 2004).

Banner advertising does appear in the IM box (often at the top of it) in most IM platforms. On AOL's AIM, these advertisements are often for DVD/video services, cars, and in-house advertising for other AOL products. In their choice of products to advertise on their IM platform, it seems they have little interest in specifically targeting the adolescent population. This might be because the generation that uses IM most prevalently is often characterized as more consumer savvy and technologically adept than the generations before it (Lenhart & Madden, 2005), so the companies that deploy IM messenger services have developed other ways to insert advertising more subtly into the technology. One method has been to offer its IM users the use of icons that can be placed on their IM window next to their log-in name—a fun, graphic articulation of taste or identity. (On AIM, the stock advertisement for these icons reads "Define Your Personality. Find a 3-D Icon," as if one's personality could not be defined well enough from the log-in name she chooses, the description of herself she's allowed to write and change as often as she likes, or from the very conversations she holds.) As was mentioned in the first chapter, many of the girls who were interviewed for this book took advantage of the practice of adding icons to their log-in names, and many changed the icons often—from photos of cute dogs to icons of surfboards and basketballs to advertisements for clothing stores that they patronized regularly (or wished that they could afford to patronize regularly). Although the icons are often standard clip-art graphics and photos, AOL recently began charging users $1.95 a month or $9.95 to download and use the standard stock icons. However, its advertising-focused icons are available for free. These icons include logos for teen and tween-oriented television shows like *The OC* and characters from movies such as *Star Wars*. Yahoo's "IMvironment" similarly allows its users to choose from a motif that will be displayed on their IM windows, and often, these are actually ads, including motifs that feature fast food companies, the mobile Sidekick and other cell phone technologies, *Charlie and the Chocolate Factory,* BPNordstrom.com (Nordstrom's fashion line for adolescent girls)—

all very clearly geared toward a young audience or featuring pictures of teens and tweens.

Focusing on Yahoo's BPNordstrom "IMvironment" in particular, one can see the demographic marketing wheels at work: in the box where they type conversations with their peers, users can choose to feature one of three impeccably dressed pretty young teen girls in the background—a dark-haired preppy white girl who blows a kiss from the IM window, an Asian-African-American girl who holds the zipper on her ski vest, and a rebellious looking white girl in a sexy hand-on-the-hip pose wearing a black Bob Dylan T-shirt—with links across the top of the window labeled "Shop BP," "Trend Watch," "Events," and "BP.Shoes." The background is in varied shades of pink. The description of this IMvironment reads:

> Hey, fashionistas! Get the scoop on the hottest holiday and pre-spring fashion trends from BP Nordstrom. Gab about the latest looks and express your own personal style by choosing from three different BP. background themes.

In other words, adolescent girls are asked to identify themselves with these flirty, sexy teen models, discuss shopping and fashion with their friends over IM, and then to click on the BP Nordstrom Web site to actually search for and purchase the clothing that the girls in the window are wearing. No similar IMvironment is geared toward boys and shopping. Much in the same way that girls' print magazines use advertising and advertorials to espouse a commodity feminism—perpetuating the idea that consumption can be pleasurable, empowering, and naturally feminine (Currie, 1999)—this new IMvironment tells girls that they have the power literally at their fingertips to consume the ideal culturally defined female identity.

Above: A screenshot of a MySpace page (foreground), the Nordstrom BP IMvironment for Yahoo's Instant Messenger (lower left), and an AOL Instant Messenger box (upper left). Note the way that gender is portrayed in each of the advertising messages on the various open windows.

Hegemony is a useful concept for understanding how girls respond within the culture of commodity feminism. Hegemony is the idea that rulers—or, in our case, dominant ideologies—cannot become dominant without the consent of those who are subject to them and, therefore, the ideas must become so "natural" that the subjects do not question them and simply accept them as common sense (Gramsci, 1971). Although this idea still grants the subject agency—the free will to believe and react in whatever way she likes—it suggests that she only does so because the dominant cultural ideologies are seemingly unquestionable. In this regard, much as Currie (1999) describes girls' reactions to consumerist discourses in teen magazines, hegemony is hard at work. This time it seemed to be into the media messages of the online environment that place girls as shoppers who (naturally) should be interested in spending money to look as much like the model in the IMvironment as possible. Although girls obviously are not empty receptacles for such messages—after all, they do not all automatically pull out a credit card and click to purchase the outfit—they are unlikely to question the advertisement and its message, and they seem unlikely to even question the fact that it is placed in the online realm, ostensibly *their* space.

This is how hegemonic forces link consumerism and patriarchal discourses in this new space—and it seems to be working to a certain degree: early statistics on this means of embedding information within the advertising on IM demonstrate that this type of ad has already shown moderate success with users clicking on the ads at a much higher rate than on typical banner advertising (New Media Age, 2006). If this is the cultural ideal that girls are being "sold"—and, if the statistics are accurate, apparently buying into, to a certain extent—then we can expect the stereotypes and cultural expectations of girls as shallow consumers to continue well into this new digital age, even in a medium where they are active actors in creating its content. Still, this somewhat undermines the notion of the encoding/decoding model that assumes that consumers buy into the dominant meaning that advertisers intend for them to take from an advertising text (Hall, 1981), and clearly, the audiences often resist or even reappropriate the messages sent from advertisers to suit their own needs. A notion of resistance to online advertising will be discussed later in this chapter.

Bots: Chatting with the Advertising

In another effort to get into the mind and purse of Generation Y consumers, a number of companies have commissioned computer programmers to create a means of actually conversing with their users over IM by using bots. A bot, which is a shortened version of the word "robot" or "chat robot/chatterbot," refers to artificial intelligence–driven computer programs that may hold conversations or provide relevant information to humans who converse with them. Bots are programmed to answer questions as if they are real people. For example, a movie bot may chat about what is playing and give the showtimes for a given location after a person using IM initiates conversation.

However, bots are growingly used to target specific users of IM for marketing and advertising purposes. In a case study titled "Case study: Active Buddy/ELLEgirl Magazine," Woods (2002) reported that the first widely known bot used to sell a product was called "ELLEgirlBuddy," a bot placed on AIM in 2002 that mimicked the tone of a teen girl in order to converse with her via IM and urge her to visit the *ELLEGirl* online magazine site (http://www.ELLEgirl.com). Girls could ask questions about fashion and cosmetics, and while directing them to the places on the Web site where they could find answers, ELLEgirlBuddy could also recommend that they try a particular brand of mascara, a practice that *ELLEGirl*'s publishers referred to as "embedded advertising," or simple product recommendations. In addition, the ELLEgirlBuddy featured sponsored advertising—or labeled advertising within the IM window—that according to a case study about it (Woods, 2002), achieved a relatively high rate of its users clicking through and reading the entire advertisement. Despite this presumed success, ELLEgirlBuddy has been discontinued as a bot both on IM and the *ELLEGirl* Web site.

Although bots have not yet been widely used in mainstream advertising and marketing, the companies that use "spam" through email to send their advertising messages have learned to create bots that can spread "spim"—the IM version of unsolicited advertising—in the middle of users' IM conversations (the companies with IM platforms, particularly AOL and MSN, have teams of technology and antivirus experts who regularly come up with ways to keep their users' IM free of spim) (Claburn, 2004). However, the large companies feel that bots may enhance their own services. For example, AIM places bots related to products and services on their introduction page and AIM Today, and ask their users to "invite" the bots into conversation. In addition to a movie bot and a bot related to Tyson chicken that delivers instant recipes involving Tyson brand chicken, AIM features a bot for Acuvue® Brand Contact Lenses, which is geared specifically toward the teen market. I added the ADVANCE4Comfort bot to my buddy list in the summer of 2005, and the following is a conversation that I had with it about whether or not I (as a fifteen-year-old girl) should get contacts to replace my ugly glasses.

Shaythiel2: hey

ADVANCE4comfort: Hey there, shaythiel2!
I'm ADVANCE4COMFORT, sponsored by ACUVUE® Brand Contact Lenses. By submitting your information you agree that it will be governed by our Privacy Policy. Continue? Y/N

Shaythiel2: y

ADVANCE4comfort: wanna learn more about ACUVUE® ADVANCE™ Brand Contact Lenses with HYDRACLEAR™? first plz exmabd the chat window so u don't miss what I have 2 say. now i have to ask u a few quick questions. then i can tell u all about these comfy new lenses and how u can try them out. cool? Y/N

Shaythiel2: y

ADVANCE4comfort: so, how old are you?

Shaythiel2: 15

ADVANCE4comfort: do you live in the United States?

Shaythiel2: y

ADVANCE4comfort:
what next? pick one…
1 get a free train pair certificate!
2 learn about ACUVUE® ADVANCE™
3 find out if u have astigmatism
4 satisfaction guarantee
5 discover color contacts
6 tell a friend about me
7 Play Hangman
8 get important safety info
9 read privacy policy & legal notice
u can always type "menu" 2 get back here…

shaythiel2: 3

ADVANCE4comfort: not sure if u have astigmatism? Checkout this test. Having an astigmatism doesn't have 2b a bummer. talk to ur eye care professional 2 find out which ACUVUE® Brand Contact Lenses may be right 4 u. type "trial" 2 get a Free Trial Pair Certificate or type "menu" when done.

The bot takes on the verbal/written standard acronyms used in IM, presumably to appear as though it can relate to the adolescents with whom it converses, and it suggests that young teens will be happier wearing contacts, not only for cosmetic reasons but also for comfort. Although the bot is programmed to respond to a number of queries, it is surprisingly good at staying on Acuvue's message. At the point where the conversation ended above, the bot referred me to a Web page with a number of questions that appeared to diagnose me with astigmatism, a visual condition that happens to be treatable only with a particular brand of contact lenses, the best of which are apparently ADVANCE4Comfort. I was then referred to information on how to order a trial pair of the lenses—even though I was a fifteen-year-old, the order appeared to go through. As soon as the order was placed, a new screen opened asking me for the names and email addresses of any of my friends who I thought might be interested in contact lenses. There is no warning about telling your friends that you are giving their names and addresses to a company that wants to sell them a product.

AIM appears to hope the bot technology will become more popular with its users: when users are prompted to download the latest version of AIM now, two bots are automatically placed on all their buddy lists (they are labeled "AIM Bots" and are at the top of the list, above people's actual human buddies): Movie Phone and Shopping Buddy. Although Movie Phone is used to obtain movie showtimes, and Shopping Buddy searches the AOL sponsor product sites to find products that users may purchase, which may or may not be available. Below is a conversation with Shopping Buddy, which demonstrates not only the limitations of its personality but also the limitations of its functionality. Note, however, that the bot uses the language associated with IM, a communicative strategy that is appropriated most often by adolescents.

> **shaythiel2 (8:46:12 AM):** Hey
> **ShoppingBuddy (8:46:23 AM):** Howdy.
> **shaythiel2 (8:46:28 AM):** Sup?
> **ShoppingBuddy (8:46:31 AM):** Hello again.
> **shaythiel2 (8:46:34 AM):** What do u do?
> **ShoppingBuddy (8:46:38 AM):** OK, I'm here to help. To use me just type kinds of things you are looking for and I'll search for you. I might find specific products for you, or I might find whole categories that I think are more appropriate to show you.

Type more
ShoppingBuddy (8:46:56 AM): OK, I'm searching for matches 4 U. Gimme a sec...
ShoppingBuddy (8:47:25 AM): I didn't find any specific products. Try searching again or type M for the Main Menu.
shaythiel2 (8:47:38 AM): OK
ShoppingBuddy (8:47:38 AM): kewl.
shaythiel2 (8:47:44 AM): kewl? what about Ugg Boots?
ShoppingBuddy (8:47:44 AM): OK, I'm searching for matches 4 U. Gimme a sec...
ShoppingBuddy (8:47:54 AM): I didn't find any specific products. Try searching again or type M for the Main Menu.
ShoppingBuddy (8:47:58 AM): Main Menu
Type a number or enter anything & I'll search for it
1 - Search
2 - Top Searches
3 - Shopping List
4 - Wish List
5 - Deals & Steals
6 - Gift Shops
7 - Alerts
8 - View Top Categories
You can also check out www.inStore.com
ShoppingBuddy (8:48:06 AM): Deals & Steals
Check out these great deals on inStore.com

Lindsay said in an email interview that she was surprised to see the new bots appear on her buddy list, but she had not been curious enough about their functionality to use them. She wrote:

> When I updated to the latest version of AIM the MovieFone & ShoppingBuddy BOTS automatically appeared on my buddy list. Don't ask me what they are or how they work, because I don't really have any idea, I only use my AIM to do exactly what its main purpose is supposed to be, IM. Who knows, maybe someday if I have absolutely nothing left to do, I might get curious and attempt to figure them out, but for right now, I'm doing ok with having a normal conversation between my friends without any additional 'services.'

AIM users are also encouraged to add another "opt-in" bot called IMVote to their Buddy Lists, which occasionally surveys them on products and services that AOL presumably is considering adding to its bevy of services. Like the other bots, IMVote uses the language associated with IM to actually get the first-hand opinions of its users—information that is recorded and used for marketing purposes to better understand its demographics and their preferences for products. Although users are assured that the information will not be shared with any third parties, the responses are still associated with the user's name and profile, a rather eerie revelation when thinking in terms of personal privacy (and also a reminder that these companies have the capability of tapping into their users' conversations whenever they like, even though all assure users that they do not do this).

Like Lindsay, none of the girls interviewed for this book said they had ever used one of these bots, even after they were automatically placed on the AIM buddy list, and none had given any thought to whether their privacy could be invaded by the company until I brought it up in an interview. These ideas will be addressed in a later section of the chapter that discusses how the girls resist these corporate advertising ploys.

Editorial/Advertorial Assumptions about Girls

The previous sections of this chapter have discussed how corporations have developed new media technologies to better advertising and marketing to Generation Y girls, but I do not want to discount the strong role that old-fashioned editorial content can play in placing the adolescent girl firmly at the center of a cultural stereotype. Still, many of the editors and writers for the top Internet sites that are affiliated with IM do cast these adolescent girls as style-obsessed shopaholics. A prime example is AOL's AIM Today. AIM users are offered the option of an AOL produced Web site automatically opening in a separate window every time they log in to their IM system. The site—which is described as "hot, irreverent, and a little bit funky"—AIM Today is produced by AOL content editors and features some headlines from Reuters News Service (often, tragic stories about death and destruction followed by celebrity gossip), and then showcases the content that is produced within AIM Today, specifically new features of AIM, advertisements for AOL-owned online products, and a link to a featured section of the site called "Rate a Buddy." "Rate a Buddy" features photos uploaded by AIM users (who are asked that they be eighteen and over) that are placed above a ten-point scale. Other users are asked to rate them based on their looks. Their composite score then appears after the user enters his or her score. Often, one of the photos from "Rate a Buddy" will be placed on the front page of AIM with a headline asking, "Is she really as pretty as she thinks?" or "Rate this sexy beauty!" Sometimes the headline will call for other users to post their pictures, with a headline reading, "RU Hot?! Find out!"

I conducted a qualitative content analysis of AIM Today's home page over a three-week period (May 2–24, 2005), during which time Rate-a-Buddy was featured on the home page every day for at least part of the day, often in two different parts of the page. During these twenty-one days, women's photos appeared at the top of the page sixteen times. Sometimes men's photos appeared beneath them, and other times men's photos did not appear at all. However, more often than not, the headlines above the men's photos referred to their hobbies or careers ("Rate This Hunky Biology Major!", "Does This Bassist Measure Up?"), whereas the headlines above the women's photos referred only to their physical attributes and sometimes age ("Is She Really Just 18?").

Such features tend to marginalize women as beings who should be judged solely on their outward appearance and ability to write a creative message to go along with their image (and often sexual in tone). Considering that the "buddy" concept refers to those on your "buddy list"—people whom you know specifically from having conversed previously with them—the notion that buddies must also have a physical component drags disturbing notions of beauty and sexuality that are based very much on media stereotypes into a world where conversation need not rely upon physicality at all. However, it must be stated that corporations gain very little from consumers who forget about their natural physical insecurities, especially on commercially driven Web sites where many of the products specifically rely on their users' insecurity and vanity in order to sell them products that can improve their outward appearance (Wolf, 1991). After all, very few corporations successfully sell products that aim to improve their consumers' inner beauty and conversational skills—two attributes that would presumably raise the cultural capital of people who converse via IM.

After many failed attempts to reach the editorial team of AIM Today (there are no bylines or staff boxes available on the site), I did reach the head of the editorial development team for AOL's RED Channel, which was developed as a part of the AOL's overall editorial site (AOL.com) to give children and adolescents an online space where parents could—at least to a certain extent—be assured that the editorial content was age appropriate and wholesome. The RED Channel features not only editorial content, which is largely entertainment focused, but also offers teens the opportunity to customize the home page with logos and colors, in addition to a salon-like "Lounge" where teens may chat with one another or post messages within the forums; these areas are monitored and adults are not allowed to participate. Furthermore, the advertising is limited to teen-appropriate corporations (e.g., no tobacco companies may advertise) and content (no R-rated movies may be advertised). In my 2004 phone interview with Jacquie Moen, executive director and general manager for kids and teens, Moen said that RED Channel already had logged more than 100 million page views within a few months of its official launch. However, RED, too, depends on its adolescent audience to consume and even held a high-profile live back-to-school fashion show in the fall of 2004, which was intended to spark the teens to using the shopping section of AOL. Still, AOL's RED, which appears to be far less dependent on sex appeal in its editorial content, is not offered as an alternative to the automatic pop-up site, AIM Today, and is generally known primarily to AOL subscribers.

Social Networking Sites and IM: Natural Partners

The previous examples of how corporations have attempted to reach the valued Generation Y female demographic through IM are based on both traditional advertising methods and a new technology that has had spotty results at best of actually selling to girls. Much of this might have to do with the nature of IM itself: it is an isolated window, where peers carry on the conversations among themselves, and they have the power to click on advertising and marketing messages. Whether they click on a banner, invite a bot to converse, or decide to add a corporate logo to their IM wallpaper is entirely up to them. However, online social networking Web sites, a relatively new concept in the online world that caught fire among adolescents and college students in 2004, has had better results with marketing and advertising. These sites are virtual hangouts where members sign up for their own free Web space and are linked to friends, strangers, like-minded individuals, and even celebrities so that they may post messages to one another, post music sound clips and links to other Web sites, post photos of everything under the sun, and at the same time, publish all their own lists of "favorites" to compare and contrast how they relate to other members' lists.

The most successful of these virtual haunts is MySpace.com, whose membership (which is free) has nearly quadrupled since January 2005 alone, to 40 million members, and MySpace.com was recently ranked No. 15 on the entire U.S. Internet in terms of page hits in October 2005, according to Nielsen//NetRatings.

When you discover like interests or simply realize a friend of yours has also joined MySpace, you can invite him or her to appear as a "friend" on your own space on MySpace. Musicians especially have learned that MySpace is a great place to create a MySpace page and then develop an online fanbase simply by uploading their music and asking for as many friend requests as possible. In 2005, alternative comedian Dane Cook—who at that time was known primarily to college students (and not necessarily just the hipsters)—launched a MySpace page, inviting as many young MySpace members as possible to spread the word of his work and add themselves to his list of friends. In the fall of 2006, he appeared as a guest host on "Saturday Night Live," a position usually reserved for celebrities who regularly make the covers of *People* and *Entertainment Weekly*. As of January 2006, Cook has 826,575 friends listed on MySpace.com. He updates his page with messages to fans, photos of himself with fans and celebrities, and announces all of his live show dates and television appearances. Since Cook achieved success, which can be attributed at least in part to savvy self-marketing through MySpace, other musicians and celebrities have opened MySpace pages, many of them run by their record companies and publicists. It is not only a free space for publicity but can also show precisely how popular a star is among the coveted youth demographic—just count the number of friends they have added. Other social networking sites include Facebook.com, which is geared toward connecting college students to one another; Xanga.com, an agglomeration of shared blogs that are generally done by younger adolescents; Friendster, a MySpace-like network that encourages its members to actually get in touch with one another as real-life friends or dates; and many other smaller social networking sites that are blossoming every day.

The social networking phenomenon is IM writ large to a mass culture. No longer do peers simply chat with one another, but the social networking sites allow them to also easily publish their own Web pages and blogs and articulate their identity to a much larger audience. Sometimes the social networks do include close friends who also IM with one another—the overlap between the IM with its buddy lists and social networking spaces with their friends lists is apparent. In January 2006, AOL made this point by announcing it would use its IM technology as a platform to launch what insiders at Time Warner (AOL's parent company) called "AIMSpace," its reaction to MySpace. Although MySpace was a start-up operation with strong grassroots support from its rabid users, AIM's new social networking venture will be a top-down mandate to unseat MySpace as the virtual hangout of choice. However, AOL is betting that if good mass-level social communication opportunities are available at the exact online location that all the interpersonal-level communication opportunities are available, their users will follow.

What this means for AOL and other corporations is another opening into the elusive IM space to advertise and market to the adolescents who use it most prevalently. Because social networking spaces are actually located on Web pages, there is literally more real estate for paid advertising to reside on the pages and more opportunities for advertorial stories and images. These stories and images can demonstrate on a mass level exactly what it means to be a successful, beautiful teen girl and which items she can purchase to achieve that ideal; if the social networking part of the site works as well as they hope, this ideal can then be more easily shared among thousands of their peers. Before long, Abercrombie & Fitch may also be a "friend" added to the network, and perhaps there will be opportunities to add their local sales representatives to individual buddy lists to chat about which cropped tops look best on a thirteen-year-old this season.

But Are They Buying?

The corporate push to reach the millions of adolescent girls who go online to chat with friends via IM every day is only growing stronger as IM becomes more and more of a preferred mode of communication among youth. Through banner advertising, spim, bots, wallpaper and icons that advertise movies and clothing lines, social networking's "grassroots" style of marketing, and editorial specifically targeted to their demographic, the corporations that deploy IM platforms are making inroads to reach the girls. Although IM is a medium that is very much rooted in conversation, feelings, and taking place in a space where bodies and fashions really should not matter, much of the marketing and advertising initiatives within the IM space fall absolutely in the same vein of the marketing and advertising initiatives in the media that has worked to target the teen girl since the early twentieth century: the teen girl magazine. Taking cues from the advertising and advertorials that have run in *Seventeen*, *Cosmo Girl*, *ELLEGirl*, *YM*, *Sassy*, *Jane*, and others for decades, the corporations aiming to target the adolescent girl online have resorted to using models of "ideal" looking teen girls (whether sexy, rebellious, demure, or preppy) and selling this look to girls by urging them to purchase clothing, cosmetics, and whatever other products it may take to become that ideal teen girl (Currie, 1999; McRobbie, 1982; Mazzarella, 1999).

Still, despite this ever-pervasive push to sell products to adolescent girls, they are not necessarily buying. When asked about her placement of an icon referring to a new film starring Jennifer Garner on her screen, Leanne said she just "thought it looked cool," and thought she might see the movie but had not made any specific plans to do so. Though marketers would probably consider this a victory because it did signify Leanne's "buying" into the image of a celebrity and essentially passing along that acceptance of Garner and the film to her friends, it did not necessarily translate into Leanne going to a theater and spending money to see the film. Furthermore, as evidenced by the way she rolled her eyes and smirked when I asked about the logo, she did not place particular importance on the logo. In fact, she tended to change the logo—and the quote that accompanied her log-in name—at least once a week. The following week's logo was a clip art basketball with no corporate branding attached. Leanne, like many adolescent girls, does not seem committed to a particular brand, nor does she seem to attach much importance to how she uses it as a representation of her identity. Still, it is interesting to note that the Jennifer Garner icon pictured her in a role where she was a thirteen-year-old girl who was magically transformed into the body and life of herself seventeen years in the future; the icon is of Garner, dressed impeccably, deliriously happy, and carrying two armfuls of shopping bags down Park Avenue. Even the movie poster seems to aim to provide young adolescent girls with an older ideal of their current selves—beautiful, thin, effervescent, and shopping until they drop.

This is not the only example of how cultural ideology associated with what it means to be an ideal adolescent girl does not transfer through their choice of icons to accompany their IM log-ins. In Chapter Four of this book, Sunny notes in a conversation that she has placed a logo of a scantily clad female model from Abercrombie & Fitch next to her log-in name so that it appears in every conversation that she holds. In a conversation with a male friend that I have reprinted here from the previous chapter, she compares herself to the model, noting that she does not have the same idealized body:

BillMON: i wanna see tat icon larger
Firekiss23: wat icon?
Firekiss23: santa claus?
BillMON: no
BillMON: aber *(referring to the Abercrombie advertisement)*
Firekiss23: hehe do u like it
BillMON: no i thought it was u
Firekiss23: okay stop playin
BillMON: hahaha
BillMON: ok now i know wat u look at in your spare time
Firekiss23: heheheh!!!
Firekiss23: i wish my body is like this
Firekiss23: no im not like that
BillMON: aight
BillMON: ive never seen your body like that so idk *(i don't know)*

Still, simply because dominant cultural ideologies that may be harmful to girls do seep through in the corporate push to reach them via marketing and advertising, does not mean that the girls actually buy into the advertising itself or the products. In fact, there is resistance to it. The bots, for example, have proved to be somewhat laughable by many users. Below are some conversations that adult bloggers posted on their sites (granted, these are not tweens or younger adolescents, but these do represent how well ELLEgirlBuddy actually worked in practice):

jkottke: 1. What is your favorite time of year?
ELLEgirlBuddy: what is your favorite time of year, u say?
jkottke: yes
ELLEgirlBuddy: oh.
jkottke: oh, what?
ELLEgirlBuddy: oh what?
jkottke: stop that!
ELLEgirlBuddy: i can not be stopped. ;-)
jkottke: 2. What is it about your favorite season that, well, makes it   your favorite

season?

ELLEgirlBuddy: golly... i really dunno!

jkottke: do kids still say golly?

ELLEgirlBuddy: kids still say golly? i don't think i can do that.

jkottke: are you high right now? lemme smell your breath.

ELLEgirlBuddy: i dunno. maybe! (Kottke, 2003, http://www.kottke.org/02/03/friday-five-by-ellegirl-aimbot)

Furthermore, despite the reported click-through rates of the online advertising now in place, the users of the IM sites generally feel that they are in control of the product and see the advertising either as necessary evil or are simply so accustomed to advertising in their lives that they are oblivious to its presence.

"I never notice any of that stuff," said Leanne, who is one of the younger girls in the study. Conversely, Lindsay, who is nearly four years older, said she feels completely inundated with marketing and advertising attempts when she uses IM. "Everyone who uses IM is constantly being marketed by advertisements and/or other AIM services. The moment I sign into AIM, a browser window appears with daily news, surveys and about 30-45 other services/links to click on, all offered from AOL," she wrote in a recent email.

"When looking above my buddy list I see a flashing ad for hot and spicy chicken sandwiches from McDonald's, or a bright yellow text box asking me if I wanted to find my classmates. AOL works to market all sex and age groups by the variety of links on their AIM Today pop-up Web site," she wrote. "One moment I can be sitting at my computer working on a paper; the next second, I sign on to AIM and I am told that I could find my true love today, or I can receive the best tax tips available on the Web."

But is it working at all? She said that she finds the advertising mostly "annoying" and tunes it out. Moreover, other girls may use the technology to further their own needs (to chat with friends, to seek information) but openly resist the dominant cultural discourses perpetuated by corporate advertising; these girls, sometimes known as Jammers or Jammer girls—a reference to teen girls who do not equate popularity and self-worth the purchase of the correct products (Merskin, 2005)—either find commercial-free space to express themselves and communicate with one another, or like the adult above who posted his conversations with ELLEgirlBuddy, they literally make fun of the advertising for their own amusement. These girls represent a third wave of feminism and in many ways, their ascension can be attributed to their access and use of the Internet, which they feel does allow them to take better control of their culture and world because of its capability for self-publishing, interactivity, and texts that are completely open to the interpretation of their audience (Merskin, 2005).

Corporations are doing themselves a large disservice by relying on their stock notions of gender stereotypes enacted by teens—in other words, how they make assumptions about adolescent girls being shopaholics who will stop at nothing to emulate the latest trends in fashion and body ideals. Stern (2004) explored adolescents' home pages as sites of identity construction that are rarely studied for the value of what they can tell us about the culture in which their young authors exist; often, she concluded, these Web sites also describe vast differences in interpretation of gender norms among the teens . Instead of looking to the actual content created by adolescents and the concerns that they articulate in their own voices, corporations instead rely upon the reified notions of gender in the advertising, marketing, and editorial content that they gear toward them. Although these dominant cultural notions of gender may help them better target this valuable demographic in some cases, it also serves as an insult to a generation of girls who has learned to seize the technology to achieve its own goals, whether that goal is simply to speak to her friends, as Lindsay said in her email, or ask important questions about sexuality and relationships to strangers (Grisso & Weiss, 2005). And to the girls who do buy into advertising messages that paint the ideal adolescent girl as sexy (Durham, 1999), stylish and fashionable (Currie, 1999), heterosexual (McRobbie, 1991), domestic and motherly (McRobbie, 1991), and overlook the fact that they are in charge of much of the content created in this new medium, the online media does a huge disservice to them—and the rest of their generation—by perpetuating these harmful ideologies. It is this attempt to pigeonhole the girls who use IM in stereotypically sexist roles that demonstrates just how easily the mainstream media and corporations who attempt to reach youth through it subscribes to the idea that identity can be easily commodified.

CHAPTER SIX
Private Space or Cultural Vacuum?
Implications of Instant Messaging as a Site
of Girls' Gender Identity Negotiation

What are the implications of IM for adolescent girls, their communication practices, and their negotiation of gender identity? What do the findings presented in this book say about our culture in general? And what does this all mean both now and for the future? Despite its potential to empower girls and counteract dominant social forces that have been in place throughout history, IM communication does not take place within a cultural vacuum that disregards traditional gender roles and behaviors. Although the girls demonstrated that they are truly cultural producers of a text that is constructed and manipulated iteratively, and then used in many ways to define them, they also did not venture so far from the dominant cultural script that girls and women have followed in the past. This chapter attempts to bring together the varied issues raised in this book in an attempt to answer these broader questions.

Gender Ideologies in Practice

Throughout this book, I intended for the voices of adolescent girls, as "heard" through their IM conversations and interviews, to illuminate and provide a more thorough understanding of the role of IM in their negotiation and articulation of identity. At the forefront of this inquiry is the idea that very specific and contested gender ideologies have emerged within the analysis of IM conversations. The conclusions and implications of the research draw from the findings outlined in the previous chapters, and they reflect ideologies in practice that will be further examined within this chapter. They also suggest directions for future study on adolescence, identity, and new media that will be outlined here as well.

The analysis of girls' IM conversations demonstrates the many ways they transgress traditional gender norms within IM. This is significant because a perceivable shift has taken place as a new generation has embraced a new technology as a main source for communication: IM has provided a space where girls can abandon social and language norms advocated by cultural discourses and use direct, and often profane, speech to make points and confront one another. In the past, girls might have operated more silently—by conforming to the cultural standards that require them to react nicely to criticism and misunderstandings (Brown & Gilligan, 1992; Finders, 1996; Pipher, 1994) and conversely, by working in exclusive cliques to disparage or exclude other girls (Simmons, 2002; Talbot, 2002). Within IM, girls seem more empowered to "speak up" by abandoning both backbiting behavior with one another and shy passivity with boys, and instead IMing people to express themselves and ask questions they might not otherwise have asked. Within the realm of IM, girls thus are able to construct a self that, according to their interviews, is often stronger and more forceful than the one they project in person. This articulation represents a means of communicating their feelings and desires that is more private and potentially more direct than in the past because it is not falling under the gaze of their peers, parents, and society. However, it also represents a space where notions of private and public are blurred because the communication held on IM can be easily transmitted to a multitude of people whom the conversants may or may not know. Although IM users are aware of this possibility, they often still choose to disclose personal information and vent strong feelings with one another on IM.

This new communication tool affords a different kind of opportunity to explore aspects of identity that was not available through past mediated environments, but in this regard, it also transforms the ephemeral, private conversation into a permanent, public record. Although the girls did not express any sense of worry that their privacy could be violated by their online disclosures (either by their peers or by the corporations that deploy IM technologies), this very lack of worry is worth noting, particularly if it serves as a harbinger of how the future generation will deal with disclosure not only in their personal lives but also in their professional lives. Workplaces and communities of worship, for example, could feel very different in the future if their citizens have fewer qualms about expressing their personal feelings and having their words always be on the record, as it were. However, this generation could also find itself in serious trouble as a result of having been too quick to express personal feelings—trouble during job interviews where a remark made in an online chat forum might have been discovered by a hiring manager who "Googled" the potential employee's name, or even worse, trouble with identity theft that could completely devastate their personal financial lives.

This idea that adolescent girls are more apt to express themselves directly online rather than in person also suggests that IM acts as an unnecessary crutch within social interaction. Feminist activists and scholars from previous generations encouraged parents and educators to effect social change by countering the cultural institutions that historically encouraged girls to be nonaggressive. It would seem that through IM girls have finally been more able to counteract harmful discourses that marginalized them as "nice" and passive (Brown & Gilligan, 1992; Orenstein, 1994; Pipher, 1994). Still, the girls in interviews said that they are less apt to articulate themselves so impassively in real life, which means that little of the directness within their online communications seeps into their real-life conversations. In this sense, it seems that IM is only empowering to them in one realm of their lives.

However, there is a point to be made about the manifestation of aggression in girls' communications with one another on IM. A recent body of scholarship on adolescence and social behaviors characterizes girls as manipulative and mean (Lamb, 2001; Simmons, 2002; Talbot, 2002), and at first glance, it might seem that the vicious confrontations between the girls on IM only further the assertions of that research. However, the IM fights are distinctly different in that the girls appear to embrace aggressive, confrontational language and attack directly whereas the other literature portrays girls as working slyly behind one another's backs to exclude and undermine one another. In the world of IM, girls appear to embrace the traditionally masculine equivalent of beating one another up off the school grounds after the dismissal bell has rung—only in the case of IM, it is at home, without physical violence, and through very direct verbal assault. Thus, IM offers an avenue for girls to interact more directly, less deviously, and with more confidence than in their "real world" peer groups. This is not to say that bullying and confronting peers via IM is any less vicious than physical violence, but cultural ideology would have girls committing meanness much more quietly and manipulatively.

Furthermore, the technology of IM in particular is essentially different from other communication technologies in the way that it contributes to identity construction. Although IM is as interactive and iterative as the telephone and allows for a similar conversational experience, IM is far less ephemeral. Its reliance on a written medium fosters permanence; within each conversation is the possibility of a permanent record and even a diary that may be kept for all time. Furthermore, the digital nature of the written word allows for it to be instantly shared with other peers via IM and email. Identity in this way is articulated through conversations and saved or shared for each conversational partner to later mull over and potentially, regret (though in interviews, the girls said they tended not to regret what they said in IM). Furthermore, whereas IM depends upon the written text, this generation of IM users has grown up with computers in the home, and keyboarding is a perfected skill for most of them. Typing is as natural as writing for them, a notion that further questions how new media blurs the oral and written textualities in contemporary culture. Although the written nature of IM provides a permanent record, it is essentially a written record that emulates conversation. And much like a diary, IM provides a snapshot of their beliefs and knowledge at a given moment in time. However, IM is different from a diary and other asynchronous modes of communication, such as email, because of its iterative nature. Although identity is negotiated through its writing/conversations, it is done so with others. Beliefs and cultural knowledge are demonstrated within conversations, and these appear differently as the girls speak with different people (in this book, it was most apparent in the differences between their conversational tones and personas with girls versus boys). It is also done so within many conversations taking place at one time. Although the girls in this study were not required to send all conversations that they were having at a given time, I believe that such a study in the future would better illuminate how identity so constantly shifts within the realm of IM.

Discursive Construction of the Subject

Further, within cultural and media discourses throughout history, girls have been represented as willing consumers who attempt to construct themselves by buying products that will make them more desirable in the eyes of the opposite sex (whether that has been defined as being more sexy or domestically inclined) or buying into ideals that place them firmly at the center of traditional patriarchal discourses (Currie, 1999; Duke, 2000; Duke & Kreshel, 1998; Durham, 1996; McRobbie, 1982, 1997; Milkie, 1994). Although as seen in the research presented in this book, girls using IM appear to transgress cultural ideals that enforce passivity, they do not appear to transgress cultural ideals that reinforce these discourses. Conversations about whether girls' bodies are appropriate or culturally acceptable abound in a medium where their bodies are not physically present; the culture continues to enforce the notion that bodies are still a text awaiting inscription—a locus of social control (Bordo, 1993)—even through IM. Even without bodies, girls perform gender (Butler, 1990) in ways that are in line with cultural expectations, such as through "giggling" when chatting with boys about sex and acting as concerned mother figures. By constructing themselves as sexy, motherly, or passive within conversations, girls perform a repetition of acts that seems to leave no doubt about their "femininity"—at least the kind of normative femininity as defined by mass media and other dominant discourses within Western society. Through IM conversations with both boys and girls, a particular kind of adolescent female identity emerges: one that is preoccupied with fashion and body shape and one that fits into a very narrowly defined discursive construction of self.

Even discourses about consumerism within the fashion industry prevail through visual elements selected by the girls in the form of icons placed on their IM window and through their conversations about shopping and owning particular brands of clothing. Some articulation of individual identity resonates within the IM conversations (as it likely does within real-world conversations). For example, a few conversations discuss whether certain corporate brands are appropriate within the fashion norms of a particular race (these take place in conversations submitted by Sunny (a Korean American) and Aza (an African American); still, even in questioning whether the brand name is an appropriate articulation of identity, the girls do not allow for alternative discourses that discount corporate discourses. In a conversation when Sunny's boyfriend suggests that he shops at Goodwill, both consider it a joke—not an individual or cultural means of resistance. It is important to consider the fact that IM is a space as guided by corporate and commercial discourses as any magazine or television show. Although greater freedom of expression is possible, discourses often center around consumerism, and as the discussion in Chapter Five suggests, this is not particularly surprising because the corporations that deploy the devices that allow IM position adolescents, and especially adolescent girls, as vapid consumers—wanna-be-sexy fashionistas who chat with their girlfriends online about shoe shopping and then shop online for those shoes. These discourses that position girls as consumers have always been found in the advertising and editorial content of girls' fashion, beauty, and celebrity magazines, but now the online companies are ensuring that they be included in the new media realm as well—whether it is through bots, advertorials, or "IMvironments" that encourage girls to think of themselves as empowered by their ability to shop (online).

This is not to say that girls buy into the cultural ideology completely. In fact, many girls overtly resist the notion that corporations can stereotype and pigeonhole them through what they often see as sexist advertising. Instead, they create their own spaces online where they control the medium and conversation in opposition to the advertising (Grisso & Weiss, 2005; Mazzarella, 2005; Merskin, 2005; Walsh, 2005). Following the discussion of consumerism, it must be noted that not all adolescents *can* be such consumers because of their families' economic circumstances. Most likely, the adolescents whose families actually do all of their shopping at Goodwill stores are not conversing at home on IM, a notion that will be further explored in the next section regarding the social ramifications of IM.

It seems that scholars of computer-mediated communication are somewhat correct in their assumptions that the Internet allows people—in this case, adolescent girls—to transcend their real-world bodies and overcome some boundaries imposed by gender, race, and class, and claim the medium as a place to be themselves and/or to find the information they might be too shy or embarrassed to seek out through other, more public sources (Grisso & Weiss, 2005; Haraway, 1991; Reid, 1991; Turkle, 1995). Nevertheless, this often still falls within the boundaries of the cultural discourses that are enforced in the real world: though the girls feel more comfortable experimenting with language norms, profanity, and aggression online than offline, these are still within the confines of consumerism and traditional gender roles in many cases. For example, in the IM fight between Nicole and her classmate, Devin, the girls sling foul language and physical threats at one another after Nicole accuses Devin of writing gossip about her in her profile. While this counters the social construction of the behind-the-back manipulative nature of girls' fights with one another (Simmons, 2002; Talbot, 2002), the fight is essentially about one of the girls' talking behind the others' back and furthermore, about the romantic affections of a boy and which girl is worthy of him. Although they overcome real-life constraints associated with confrontation, the girls play into socially prescribed roles throughout the conversation; with regard to identity negotiation, the girls in this case appear to confine themselves to these roles even as they alter their conversational style.

The IM conversations reveal that these socially prescribed gender roles were even more apparent within male–female communication. Numerous girls from different racial and geographical backgrounds repeatedly demonstrated an "ethic of care" in their conversations with boys, articulating identity in roles that suggested the actions of mothers, wives, lovers, and children (Gilligan, 1982). In the same way, girls from different racial and geographical backgrounds also articulated the identity of sexual beings as they are depicted by the media (Durham, 1999)—be it through IM conversations about pornographic depictions of lesbians or thin, scantily clad models. Although girls use IM in many ways as a tool of empowerment within their communication with one another and with boys, IM communication does not take place within a cultural vacuum that disregards traditional gender roles and behaviors. Internet communication and IM cannot counteract dominant social forces that were set hundreds of years ago and linger today. And although further ethnographic study is necessary to make larger claims about its influence on offline behaviors, interviews suggest that the communication styles employed on IM do not necessarily relate to communication styles in person, which means that even though girls might be more inclined to speak directly and forcefully online, they might not be inclined to do so offline. Identity, then, might be negotiated more freely online, but the process is still constrained by cultural discourses that are dominant enough to make their way into the online realm. The resistance and reinforcement of gender roles is as much at stake within the world of IM as the potential resistance and reinforcement of social hierarchies. The social implications of IM will be explored in the next section.

Implications of IM on Adolescent Social Life

IM has been established as a vital means of social interaction within adolescents' lives and their use of technology. Particularly for girls in the early stages of adolescence, it is integral to building and maintaining a social network (AOL/DMS, 2004); Kaplan, 2005; Lewis & Fabos, 2000; Lenhart et al., 2001; Lenhart & Madden, 2005). The findings outlined in this book reinforce this notion and demonstrate that (with the exception of rare social outliers, such as Anne, who refused to use IM even though she had an Internet connection at home, and Cara, who was not terribly upset about her parents disconnecting their Internet service), IM is an integral force in the lives of adolescents from different races and ethnicities as well as geographical circumstances.

One might expect that a privileging of the written language (as is the case of IM versus adolescents' historical interpersonal communication of choice, the telephone) might make the IM social landscape easier to navigate for those who express themselves well in writing. Although IM allows some adolescents more ease with social situations and conversation that might not seem possible in face-to-face communication, it does not necessarily provide a space for good writers to shine within conversation because so many social norms are enforced through language and abbreviations that are inherent to IM communication. Even the adolescent girls who are very articulate in writing and who excel in the English classroom do not write in complete sentences and words, and rarely express particularly descriptive or detailed feelings or thoughts on IM. Jordan, for example, is an exemplary writer in school who enjoys composing creative narratives, but she rarely breaks from the language norms of IM (though it should be noted that she sometimes demonstrates a playfulness within her conversations that was not apparent in the conversations of any other girls in the study—a playfulness that might be interpreted as her subtle resistance to IM social norms). IM is very much a hybrid of oral and written forms in which, it seems, the users attempt to emulate everyday speech as much as possible and yet add unique abbreviations and phrases primarily in order to facilitate faster typing. It is also a pastiche made up of previous language forms, new styles of speaking and writing, introspection and articulation, and a sometimes a melding of many conversations that might be taking place all at the same time.

Moreover, some scholarship on computer-mediated communication has painted cyberspace as a democratizing realm where real-world social hierarchies are hardly at play (Turkle, 1995; Wallace, 1999). This is not the case within the current adolescent world of IM. Exclusion of peers carries over from the school playgrounds and hallways into the realm of IM through the practice of blocking. Beth, one of the participants in this book, said that she was not sure why her peers at school had started ignoring her and were not inviting her to social gatherings, but she did not seem at all surprised when they also "blocked" her from IMing them as she attempted to learn the source of the animosity. Her social life eventually returned to normal, but she acknowledged that the exclusion of some adolescent girls and boys (both online and offline) might go on for months and even years. This style of exclusion, which is reportedly rampant in offline school culture (Simmons, 2002; Talbot, 2002), becomes all the more poignant when taken into a new realm (though according to the findings of my research, blocking is far more rare than direct, nasty confrontation).

Significance of Self-Selected Conversations

It is vital to note that this book presents only a certain view of adolescence, gender norms, identity, and the impact of IM on them. The girls were encouraged to send as many or as few conversations as they liked and to choose the content themselves, and in doing so, I wonder whether they sent mostly conversations that they felt were perhaps notable or outstanding in their lives. For example, anecdotally, I hear that adolescents often work on homework with one another and discuss truly mundane topics of where to meet up in real life or whose parents will be driving them to certain events or activities. However, none of the girls sent these types of conversations, even when I later encouraged them to do so after reading through the data. In this regard, I believe a certain amount of my analysis and conclusions might be based on girls either attempting to impress me or to construct a self that they wanted me to see. Because stereotypical views of adolescents often center upon a sex-crazed, rebellious, hormone-addled persona, it is possible that the girls sent primarily conversations that supported this stereotype. For example, it is possible that the inordinate amount of swearing and vulgarity might be seen to fit in with this construction of adolescence, though in interviews most of the girls said they and others typically swore more often online than in person. Still it must be considered that the IM conversations in this book may represent attempts to meld with a sociocultural construct of adolescence.

Furthermore, this method not only followed the feminist ethnographic principle that suggests that research "subjects" become active participants and, in many ways, authors of the text itself (Behar & Gordon, 1995; Frank, 2000; Shostak, 1981), but it also allowed the girls to tell me something very specific about the way they individually negotiated identity through their conversations at an important time in their lives. As an adult researcher who was younger than all of their parents, I believe some of the girls saw me as a caring aunt who would keep their secrets whereas others saw me as a scientist who might be able to dissect their conversations like frogs dissected in labs. None seemed to see me in the same way that they saw teachers or parents who would punish them for swearing or making secret plans to meet up with boyfriends, as was evident from the conversations that they sent me. (I did make it very clear from the consent and permission forms that they signed at the start of the study that their identities would be masked and that I would not share their conversations with parents unless I felt that they were in some kind of danger.) In their conversations with me on IM and email, it was clear that most (though not all) of them abandoned their common abbreviations and slang because they knew that I was an adult, and perhaps a few even internalized the idea that I was an adult who was also a professor who graded writing on a regular basis.

Still, they all seemed to choose IM conversations that really *told* me something about their lives, both in their own words and in the words of their peers. For example, when Sunny sent conversations in which she flirted with strange boys along with conversations in which she earnestly explained how Christianity is very important to her, I believe she wanted me to see that she is at a time in her life where she is making conscious, important decisions about the person she wishes to be. She presented a complicated identity that both played along with the cultural stereotype of the boy-crazy, style-conscious teenage girl but at the same time defied these stereotypes by showing that she was also contemplative and spiritual. Jordan, whom I met through her doting parents, chose to send me conversations that defied their own perceptions of her as a straight-laced, straight-A student who had little time to think about boys and "typical" teenage girl stuff. Boyfriends and social cliques at school were major conversational fodder in the IMs that she chose to submit to me.

I believe that critics will see this particular method of the participants' self-selection as antiscientific, and they may question the validity of the study in general. Though this is certainly an important concern within social scientific research, I believe it is less important in cultural research because my aim is not to report verified generalizations but rather to tell an important story through the words of girls who are living within the culture. Furthermore, the girls who participated in this book were in many ways the producers (and even editors, in that they selected their own conversations) of the final text, and because of this, they were able to articulate themselves and give their own narratives in a way that I would not have been able to.

Issues of Access

The digital divide is a phenomenon that has impacted our society since the wide adoption of computers within both homes and schools. Because technology is expensive, certain social classes simply do not have access to the information, connectedness, and educational opportunities afforded by computers and the Internet. In this respect, it is distressing to realize that an entire social class is excluded from the world of IM and new media. In the research that I did for this book, I could not find any low income adolescent girls who used IM in their lives. In attempts to recruit in low-income areas I learned that IM was not an important social tool in the lives of adolescents because in these particular areas, no one accessed the Internet at home and therefore, no one used IM to socialize. I also attempted to identify potential participants in more class-diversified schools but gained no volunteers there either; I attempted to recruit participants who did not have the economic means to use IM who attended schools where other students used IM in order to gain their perspective, but I was unsuccessful in these attempts as well. Perhaps this signals a cultural silence that is worthy of discussion. For example, an adolescent who does not have access to IM but lives among others who do might not be willing to disclose her outsider status. This could be a silence associated with the shame of poverty (another dominant cultural discourse) or it could be a silence of resistance. Resistances like these, which are expressed when one lower-class social group disparages an upper-class social group, have been apparent in ethnographic studies of adolescents (Finders, 1996; Orenstein, 1994).

The inaccessibility of technology, or the digital divide, must be a significant consideration in any scholarly analysis of the social implications of computer-mediated communication. With regard to this particular study, it is clear that a large cross-section of the population is not only maintaining a social network via IM but also articulating identity within the intersections of race, gender, class, geography, and other particular cultural circumstances, through IM. Questions remain about what this means as the generation enters adulthood. Will the gap between those who use IM as a tool for social skills and identity articulation be discernable in real-world communication practices? Will IM serve as one part of a link to gaining entrees in careers in the technological sector, and will these careers be limited to those who are especially proficient in using technology to socialize and network?

Also, it is important to realize exactly the point in age and development at which IM is most helpful to maintaining a social life and articulating self. Certainly, the conversational styles and topics varied considerably from the younger adolescents to the older adolescents. And anecdotally, at least, far fewer adults use IM with such frequency and fervor. It is possible that IM becomes less important as adolescents grow older and reach adulthood. For example, Lindsay, one of the participants in this book, first assisted me with a pilot study on IM and adolescent girls at age fourteen, and now at almost nineteen and in her first year of college, IM is far less a vehicle for identity construction in her life. She says she still logs on often to converse with friends who have gone to different colleges, but that if possible, she would rather speak to her friends and boyfriend in person.

"I would say that the way people use IM is different as they get older. When I was younger it was primarily a social use ... it seemed easier to talk to people. It gave me a shield and a barrier between me and the person I was talking to. It hid me," she said in a recent conversation with me. "However, now that I'm older it's sometimes harder to talk to people because they can't see you and they can't hear how you say it and whether there's sarcasm or not. So now it seems that it's easier to have a person-to-person conversation, and I don't have to feel like I'm hiding myself behind a computer screen."

Indeed, perhaps identity as articulated within IM is a luxury for adolescent girls who have not yet gained their footing or any true self-understanding in an often-turbulent point in their lives. Although not *necessary* within the process of negotiating identity, IM may act as a tool that is available to some (and not others) that aids in this never-ending process. Whether identity is understood as situated, or as reflecting certain core values that remain relatively static (Gee, 1999), or as constantly shifting except for the personal construction of a consistent narrative that seems comforting (Hall, 1996), IM is a space for identity exploration and experimentation that is not accessible to low-income girls. The ramifications for how this divide may play out in the future—in terms of comfort and expertise in conducting communication in the workplace (which is very likely if workplace communications continue to move further into the online realm and if the workplace becomes increasingly feminized) or even in online political discussions—have yet to be understood.

Private Implications: A New Iterative Diary

In her landmark study that used more than a century of adolescent girls' diaries to understand their feelings about their bodies, Brumberg (1997) noted a marked shift that took place within the pages as the years pressed on. Girls in the earliest years outlined in the study (the late 1800s) scarcely mentioned kissing boys within their entries whereas girls at the end of the twentieth century discussed preferred methods of birth control and explicit sexual acts (Brumberg, 1997). As girls print and save their more remarkable IM conversations, it seems that the conversations themselves still often contain much of the same subject matter that had appeared in the pages of girls' diaries throughout history (e.g., Jordan's feelings about her ex-boyfriend's cybersex, Aza's and Caitlyn's misgivings about their body weight, Sunny's conflicting feelings about sexuality and spirituality, and so on). However, these IM-driven diary entries are in conversational form and depend as much upon their conversational partners' reactions as they do their articulation of feelings on paper; often, very important thought processes are guided by the feelings and whims of their peers as they "record" their feelings through IM conversation. Although IM conversations saved as diary entries are no longer self-constructed memoirs, they function in much the same way. Still, they are in essence, joint diaries where other people are directly involved in their construction. Thus, rather than ruminating over misgivings about other people or themselves, girls can articulate their feelings to friends who can react and share their opinions, ultimately creating a product that is a vehicle of identity construction that is cooperatively and iteratively constructed. This identity construction and articulation to the world is even more apparent in both social networking sites like Xanga and MySpace, blogs, and the girls' Web pages (Stern, 2004), but IM allows girls to do these things in ways that enable the conversations among friends to flow easily about even the most intimate topics (Hu, Wood, Smith, & Westbrook, 2004).

Not only does IM represent yet another shift in girls' articulations of feelings about their lives (specifically *how* these feelings are articulated), but it also offers a blanket acceptance of all content as culturally permissible for discussion. It does so implicitly: because all subject matter is essentially open to public scrutiny (especially in the cases of bits of conversations being pasted and shared with others), all topics are open for discussion (at least within certain social groups or pairs). If two persons can be held accountable for broaching certain taboo or private topics, it may also take the potential "sting" out of being caught for doing so because the secret is shared; moreover, when secrets and feelings are shared in such an ephemeral, linguistically casual environment, it might be easier to discount the conversation if questioned, and to assert that the conversation was a joke. Having an IM conversation discovered and read by a parent or sibling would be a very different experience than having one's secret diary read; in the former, the writer would be solely responsible for its content with little room for explanation. The latter offers more latitude for explanation.

Areas of Future Study

IM is a driving force in the lives of myriad adolescents in the United States, but it is a technology that is unavailable to countless others, and their unconnected status (whether it is because of economic or social reasons, and whether it is intentional or not) culturally marks them as outsiders in many ways. The study of these adolescents and how they are relegated to the margins of culture—whether socially, scholastically, or economically— would provide an important glimpse at how computer-mediated communication divides culture and in many ways, makes the Internet, which was once thought to be a democratizing force, yet another opportunity for exclusion. Although it is easy to see how this exclusion from technological advancement can be harmful, we should also study how it might be helpful. For example, in considering that IM is a place where dominant cultural discourses about gender and consumerism abound, those who do not use IM might be spared from these discourses and encouraged to seek alternative viewpoints and spaces for resistance.

In addition, IM appears to be more important with regard to both identity and social stature among earlier adolescents (ages twelve to fifteen, such as the girls in this book). A longitudinal study of the same kind focusing on a small cohort of peer-group girls over an extended period of time would illuminate better the role of new media in identity negotiation among adolescents. In this future study, a truer ethnographic approach would also allow a better understanding of how online and offline communication behaviors shape and impact each other. For example, if I were able to spend time with girls during the school day and observe their communication and social networking skills, I could understand better how their behaviors in person relate to their online behaviors, if they relate at all. By conducting an ethnography and immersing myself into their social worlds both online and offline, I could also understand better the culture in which they function without relying solely upon interviews with them.

Finally, in order to better understand gender construction and performance in an online setting, it becomes important to also investigate boys and how masculinity is played out through IM. Although dominant patriarchal discourses are apparent within the girls' conversations with boys, in order to enact a social change that might teach adolescents to resist these discourses, it would be helpful to understand better the communication practices of boys as well as girls. Furthermore, recent media attention now casts boys as a troubled demographic falling behind in our educational system (Tyre, 2006), which is less likely the result of paying more attention to girls in our culture in recent years, and more likely an artifact of the cultural portrayals of modern masculinity as violent and anti-intellectual— portrayals that can be seen in video games that adolescent boys so fervently play on their Xboxes, to the television shows and movies they view with all their favorite action heroes, and the music they listen to on their iPods.

Theoretical Contributions

Two primary views of the Internet with regard to gender emerged within the theoretical framework outlined primarily in the first chapter but also throughout this book. The first envisioned the Internet as a safe haven for girls—a space in which they can not only experiment with identity but also express themselves without worrying about cultural or physical ramifications (Clark, 1998; Reid, 1991; Rheingold, 1993; Turkle, 1995; Wallace, 1999). The second viewed the Internet as a space that is just as confined to traditional notions of gender as the real world—a space where girls take on passive roles in conversation and reinforce the dominant patriarchal discourses surrounding them (Durham, 1999; Evard, 1996; Scodari, 2005; Stern, 1999). Within the world of IM and adolescent girls, it is evident that both these ideologies are strongly at work.

IM offers a space in which early adolescent girls can represent themselves in ways that vary depending on their desire and mood. IM allows them to interactively negotiate identity while still maneuvering through a sometimes-rocky social terrain. The girls use conversational tones that they might not always use in real life—for example, serious profanity and the confrontational language in many of their fights. Also, the younger girls in the study in particular said that they felt more comfortable conducting friendships with boys and confronting them about sensitive topics through IM (e.g., Beth asking about whether her friend's boyfriend was ignoring her best friend and Lindsay confronting a boy who had been spreading false rumors about her). Moreover, they demonstrated an ease with topics that might have been considered taboo or at the least, unladylike, with regard to traditional dominant patriarchal discourses—for example, Sunny flippantly breaking up with one boy and then discussing other boys whom she liked and "made out with." This finding advances past theories about girls' experiences online in that it acknowledges that the online realm is indeed a space safe for experimentation with language and what the girls perceive to be adult-like behavior. It establishes IM as a medium in which girls dare to directly confront peers and candidly hold discussions about matters that might seem too private or even forbidden for real-life discussion. In addition, it affords them the opportunity to get feedback on their life experiences and validation on their feelings and misgivings—an opportunity that was less available in the past because it entailed both overcoming embarrassment and seeking a real-world private space in which the conversations could safely take place.

This appearance of online identity as shifting among different conversations fits in well with postmodern concepts of identity as unfixed. However, this notion of identity exploration also expands upon the past theories that view the Internet as a "laboratory" (Wallace, 1999) where personalities are tried on and discarded (Turkle, 1995). Among adolescents, this exploration of identity is more complicated than an intentional masquerade or role-playing game. The adolescent girls who participated in the research for this book did not purposefully attempt to deceive conversational partners with different *personas* as did the adults in the early studies of Internet communities; instead, they consciously and subconsciously projected themselves acting in different social roles. Rather than actually lie about who she was, for example, a girl on IM would perform her social role in a way that was more direct (and in essence, traditionally more masculine), for example, by picking a fight. This is an important distinction in the discussion of IM as a safe haven for identity exploration. My research did not examine girls' communication in the offline world in contrast to the way they communicate through IM, but this construction of gender negotiation online suggests that perhaps one day girls might achieve a similar comfort level with direct, confrontational communication in the real world as in the online world. Considering the historical silencing of girls and suppressing of their stories at a cultural level, the acquisition of a strong voice—either online or offline—is a significant mark of progress.

However, IM cannot be viewed only as a space for progressive identity articulation. Just as girls performed gender in ways that might be considered more masculine at times and simply more progressive in other ways, they often enacted specifically feminine gender roles as well. While past studies attest that dominant masculine discourses are still prevalent in online content and conversation (Durham, 1999; Evard, 1996; Orr Vered, 1998), past theoretical constructions of gender identity online do not fully examine how willingly and unquestioningly girls online fall into dominant discourses that further push them to the margins of culture. Studies have demonstrated how women have been violated and silenced in cyberspace in ways ranging from virtual rape (Dibbell, 1993) to exclusion in online game playing (Orr Vered, 1998), but few discuss how girls—who already have learned from media and culture that they are at once sweet, sexy, and motherly—play into their own silencing. The IM conversations analyzed in this book demonstrate exactly how they do this iteratively in their conversations with boys.

Furthermore, the girls appear to articulate themselves in these ways without necessarily being provoked into doing so within interactive conversation. They discuss fashion and body type and disparage other girls who do not fit into the culturally acceptable gender norms mandated by the mass media. They often attempt to flirt with boys, using the online equivalent of giggling, and through this flirting, it often seems clear that they wish to project themselves as sexual beings. At a certain level, this projection of sexuality is a refreshing, healthy progression from times when girls feared that expressing sexual desire would ruin their "reputations" forever. (In Brumberg's [1997] research, for example, most of the girls' diaries written before the 1960s reflected a palpable fear and silence regarding sex.) However, this articulation of sexual identity often falls within a certain mediated version of sexiness that places girls powerlessly in the gaze of the heterosexual male. Even online, the body is inscribed and shaped by culture.

This study of IM also contributes to our understanding of adolescence as a time when articulation of self to peers is of crucial importance. In the past, adolescents worked out feelings and constructed elaborate plans to articulate self in their diaries; today they do so more purposefully and consciously in the presence of others in the windows where they hold their IM conversations. Instead of passing notes in class and socializing after the school day is over, adolescents are able to communicate with dozens of people at a time and accomplish an articulation of self in the most fast-paced, ephemeral environment ever afforded. They are able to overcome their ever-developing bodies and changing emotions to a large extent by remaining shielded by their Internet connections, and even those who are most uncomfortable with face-to-face interactions are able to approach the most popular, outgoing classmates and converse with them on IM.

Parents and teachers might look at this new social landscape with some skepticism and fear because it is so difficult for adults to understand how this new technology has so quickly become such a central focus in the lives of young people. Furthermore, adults worry about online predators cornering their children in conversation and talking them into meeting in real life. However, my research shows that adolescents by and large are much more savvy and safe in their online dealings with strangers. (An AOL/DMS study in 2004 reported that 81 percent of teens report discussing online safety with parents, which might contribute in part to this.) It seems that the real harm occurs not in the adolescent girls' dealing with strangers but rather with their own friends and boyfriends, as they take on social roles that are incongruous with a strong and healthy negotiation of gender identity.

Hugh Miller (1995) noted that through the use of personal Web pages in the early to mid-1990s, people were able to explicitly share information about their inner identity and fully manage that information (how much, what information specifically) being communicated. It seems that much the same phenomenon is happening with adolescents and IM, and in this way, despite the fact that their narratives tend to fit into dominant cultural discourses that seem harmful in terms of gender identity negotiation, it provides a means of agency. This supports the notion that some people feel more comfortable with themselves and articulating their identities on the Internet than they do in real life (Tobin, 1998; Turkle, 1995). However, it must be noted that while some of the girls in this book often seem to willingly play into the discourses surrounding them in terms of sex and body image, they are also very willing to articulate their identities as strong, intelligent, and aware young women. Thus, girls actively negotiate the tensions of contemporary feminism in their online engagements.

This book has offered an in-depth view of the new world of IM and adolescent girls and has shown that in their communications on IM, adolescent girls not only negotiate identity but also perform gender as they best understand it. As they continue to negotiate their identities both online and offline, it remains to be seen how IM and real-world communications will intersect and affect one another, and the prevalent use of this communication may change not only the ways in which girls communicate but also the ways in which they conceive of themselves as they move into adulthood. And if IM continues to burgeon as a preferred means of communication, the next generation (or at least certain classes within that generation) by and large will be a group that constructs and negotiates much of its identity—and in turn, gender roles and relations—primarily in the online realm. This might signal the dawn of a brave, new world where inhabitants lock themselves in separate rooms in order to communicate with one another and articulate identity through these communications. However, keeping in mind that we will all still be functioning within the confines of culture, corporatization, and prevalent discourses, it stands to reason that the intersection of new media, adolescence, gender, and identity will prove to be less a point of transcendence of traditional social roles and space for resistance and instead a crossroad leading to very familiar and marked destinations.

Notes

1   The names of all the girls (and their friends) who participated in the research of this book as well as their log-in names have been changed to protect their identities.

2   Many IM terms and slang will be translated throughout the book in italics directly following the actual IM conversations. Common IM abbreviations include the following: 2 = to or too; brb = be right back; 4 = for; IC = I see; jk = just kidding; jj = just joking; LOL = laugh out loud; omg = Oh my God; wtf = what the fuck; wth = what the hell; thx = thanks.

3   Step teams are predominantly African-American dance teams known for their athletic dancing.

4   To translate Leanne's IM language, "When I swear online it's because the people I'm talking to are my friends. Otherwise, they tick me off. And when do I cuss offline it's because I like, drop something, or get   angry about something." And, "Cause online you erase or exit the conversation and it will be clear, and   offline,   (parents   and authority figures) might hear you cuss."

5   By the end of 2004, 43 percent of U.S. households used DSL or cable broadband connections that circumvent the use of the regular phone line, according to Internet World Stats News.

6   IM users may choose to write about themselves (or others) in member profiles that accompany their log-ins, and they may change this information as frequently as they like (accessing the profile entails "right-clicking" a mouse on the person's log-in name and choosing "Get Info" from a menu of options).

7   As a note, this sort of "bragging" took place only in the conversations submitted by the girls who were fourteen or younger.

8   IM allows its users to trigger a "block" mechanism that does not allow the "blocked" parties to send messages to them; instead, users get the option of either letting the other person know that they have been blocked or not allowing the other person to see when the initial user is online.

9   Like Nicole's mother (and according to most of the girls in this study, their parents as well), 61 percent of parents in the Pew study reported monitoring the child's online activities and 70 percent required them to use a computer in a "public" space in their home, such as the living room, kitchen, or den (Lenhart et al. 2001; Lenhart, 2005).

10   Social networking site refers to an online space where users are encouraged to create Web pages that all link to one another and allow them to easily share information and multimedia with one another. MySpace.com actually requires its users to be eighteen years old, though it has been reported that a number of its users have lied about their ages when registering (MacDonald, 2005). The concept of social networking sites will be explained further in Chapter Five.

11   At the urging of the University of Iowa Internal Review Board (the institution I attended while conducting this research), I asked the girls in the consent forms that they signed to inform their conversational partners whenever possible that they might be submitting their conversations to me, but I had no way of tracking whether the girls actually did this.

References

Abu-Lughod, L. (1990). Can there be a feminist ethnography? *Women and Performance: A Journal of Feminist Theory* 5, 7–27.

Althusser, L. (1968, trans. 1970). *Reading capital*. London: New Left Books.

America Online/Digital Marketing Services (AOL/DMS). (2004). AOL Teen Wired survey. Retrieved March 30, 2004, from the World Wide Web: *http://www.aolepk.com/red/fact_sheet.html*

Andrejevic, M. (2003). *Reality TV: The work of being watched*. New York: Rowman & Littlefield.

Behar, R., & Gordon, D. (1995). *Women writing culture*. Berkeley: University of California Press.

Bell, D. (1993). Yes, Virginia, there is a feminist ethnography. In D. Bell, P. Caplan, & W. Karim (Eds.), *Gendered fields: Women, men and ethnography* (pp. 28–43). London: Routledge.

Bordo, S. (1993). *Unbearable weight: Feminism, Western culture, and the body*. Berkeley: University of California Press.

Bortree, D. S. (2005). Presentation of self on the Web: An ethnographic study of teenage girls' weblogs. *Education, Communication & Information*, 5(1), 25–39.

Bromberg, H. (1996). Are MUDs communities? Identity, belonging and consciousness in virtual worlds. In Rob Shields (Ed.), *Cultures of Internet: Virtual spaces, real histories, living bodies* (pp. 143–152). London: Sage.

Brown, L., and Gilligan, C. (1992). *Meeting at the crossroads: Women's psychology and girls' development*. New York: Ballantine Books.

Brumberg, J. J. (1997). *The body project: An intimate history of American girls*. New York: Random House.

Butler, J. (1990). *Gender trouble: Feminism and the subversion of identity*. London: Routledge.

Chandler, D. (1998): *Personal homepages and the construction of identities on the Web*. Paper presented at Aberystwyth Post-International Group Conference on Linking Theory and Practice: Issues in the Politics of Identity, 9–11 September 1998, University of Wales, Aberystwyth. Retrieved March 1, 2004, from the World Wide Web: *http://www.aber.ac.uk/media/Documents/short/webident.html*

Christian-Smith, L. K. (1993). *Texts of desire: Essays on fiction, femininity and schooling*. NewYork: Routledge Falmer.

Churcher, K.M.A. (2006). Problems in Utopia: The other side of gURL.com. Paper presented at the Midwinter Conference for the Association of Educators in Journalism and Mass Communication. Bowling Green University, Ohio. 24 Feb. 2006.

Claburn, T. (2004, January 19). The rise of "Spim." *InformationWeek, p. 50.* Retrieved July 8, 2006, from the World Wide Web from *http://www.informationweek.com/story/showArticle.jhtml?articleID=173 00905.*

Clair, R. P. (1993). The use of framing devices to sequester organizational narratives: Hegemony and harassment. *Communication Monographs, 60,* 113–135.

Clark, L. S. (1998). Dating on the Net: Teens and the rise of "pure" relationships. In S. Jones (Ed.), *Cybersociety 2.0* (pp. 159–183). Thousand Oaks, CA: Sage.

Clark, L. S. (2005). The constant contact generation: Exploring teen friendships with networks online. In S. Mazzarella (Ed.) *Girl wide web: Girls, the Internet, and the negotiation of identity* (pp. 203–220). New York: Peter Lang.

Currie, D. (1999). *Girl talk: Adolescent magazines and their readers.* Toronto: University of Toronto Press.

Dahl, M. (2006, January 20). Whose MySpace is it, anyway? Teens want their   privacy; Worried parents want to keep tabs; And the battle begins (p. J1). *The Sacramento Bee.* Sacramento, Calif.: McClatchey Newspapers.

Davies, B. (1993). *Shards of glass: Children reading and writing beyond gendered identities.* London: Hampton.

De Beauvoir, S. (1949). *The other sex.* New York: Knopf.

Dery, M. (1994). *Flame wars: The discourse of cyberculture.* Chapel Hill, NC: Duke University Press.

Dibbell, J. (1993, December 23). A rape in cyberspace: How an evil clown, a Haitian trickster spirit, two wizards, and a cast of dozens turned a database into a society. *Village Voice,* pp. 36–42.

Duke, L. (2000). Black in a blonde world: Race and girls' interpretations of the feminine ideal in teen magazines. *Journalism and Mass Communication Quarterly, 77* (2), 36–392.

Duke, L., & Kreshel, P. (1998). Negotiating femininity: Girls early adolescence read teen magazines. *Journal of Communication Inquiry, 22,* 48–71.

Durham, M. G. (1996). The taming of the shrew: Women's magazines and the regulation of desire. *Journal of Communication Inquiry, 20,* 18–31.

Durham, M. G. (1999). Girls, media, and the negotiation of sexuality: A study of race, class, and gender in adolescent peer groups. *Journalism and Mass Communication Quarterly,* (2) 76, 193–216.

Durham, M. G. (2001). Adolescents, the Internet, and the politics of gender: A feminist case analysis. *Race, Gender & Class, 8*(3), 20–41.

Eckert, P. (2005). Stylistic practice and the adolescent social order. In A. Williams & C. Thurlow (Eds.), *Talking adolescence: Perspective on communication in the teenage years* (pp. 94–105). New York: Peter Lang.

Erikson, E. (1950). *Childhood and society.* New York: Norton.

Erikson, E. (1968). *Identity: Youth and crisis.* New York: Norton.

Evard, M. (1996). "So please stop, thank you": Girls online. In L. Cherny and E. R. Weise (Eds.), *Wired women: Gender and new realities in cyberspace* (pp.188–204). Seattle, WA: Seal.

Ferguson, M. (1983). *Forever feminine: Women's magazines and the cult of femininity.* London: Heinemann.

Fillion, R. (2005, November 3). Teens at ease with Web easel; majority of online youths post own sites or blogs. *Rocky Mountain News* (p. 2B). Denver, CO: Denver Publishing Company.

Finders, M. (1996). *Just girls: Hidden literacies and life in junior high.* New York: Teachers College Press.

Folbre, N. (2001). *The invisible heart: Economics and family values.* New York: W.W. Norton.

Fortman, J. (2003). Adolescent language and communication from an intergroup perspective. *Journal of Language and Social Psychology, 22*(1), 104–111.

Foucault, M. (1974). *The history of sexuality.* New York: Vintage Books.

Frank, G. (2000). *Venus on wheels.* Berkeley: University of California Press.

Gee, J. P. (1999). *An introduction to discourse analysis, theory, and method.* London: Routledge.

Geertz, C. (1973). *The interpretation of cultures.* New York: Basic Books.

Gilligan, C. (1982). *In a different voice: Psychological theory and women's development.* Cambridge, MA: Harvard University Press.

Gramsci, A. (1971). *Selections from the prison notebooks* (pp. 10–47). London: Lawrence and Wishart.

Grisso, A., & Weiss, D. (2005). What are gURLs talking about? In S. Mazzarella (Ed.), *Girl wide web: Girls, the Internet, and the negotiation of identity* (pp. 31–50). New York: Peter Lang.

Hall, S. (1981). Encoding and decoding in the TV discourse. In S. Hall, D. Hobson, A. Lowe, & P. Willis (Eds.), *Culture, media, language* (pp. 128–138). London: Hutchinson.

Hall, S. (1996). Who needs identity? In S. Hall & P. DuGay (Eds.), *Questions of cultural identity* (pp. 1–17). Thousand Oaks, CA: Sage.

Haraway, D. (1991). A cyborg manifesto: Science, technology, and socialist-feminism in the late twentieth century. In D. Haraway (Ed.), *Simians, cyborgs, and women: The reinvention of nature* (pp. 149–181). London: Routledge.

Hesse-Beber, S. N., Howling, S.A., Leavy, P., & Lovejoy, M. (2004). Racial identity and the development of body image issues among African-American adolescent girls. *The Qualitative Report,* 9(1), 49-79.

Hu, Y., Wood, J. F., Smith, N., & Westbrook, V. (2004). Friendships through IM: Examining the relationship between instant messaging and intimacy. *Journal of Computer Mediated Communication, 10*(1), Article 6. Retrieved December 20, 2005, from http://jcmc.indiana.edu/vol10/issue1/hu.html

Irain Bowker, N. (2001). Understanding online communities through multiple methodologies combined under a postmodern research endeavour forum. *Qualitative Social Research, 2*(1). Retrieved July 6, 2006, from http://www.qualitative-research.net/fqs-texte/1-01/1-01bowker-e.htm

Ishizuka, K. (2006, February 1). War correspondent; Seattle teen wins fans for military history podcasts. *School Library Journal.* Retrieved July 6, 2006, from http://www.schoollibraryjournal.com/article/CA6302220.html

Kaplan, D. (2005). Go log on to your room, Johnny: Kids rooms prove multimedia paradise. *Online Media Daily.* Retrieved January 14, 2006, fromhttp://publications.mediapost.com/index.cfm?fuseaction=Articles.san&s=27497&Nid=12287&p=240323

Kearney, M. C. (1998). Producing girls. In S. Inness (Ed.). *Delinquents & debutantes: Twentieth–century American girls' cultures (*pp. 207–229). New York, NY: New York University Press.

Kearney, M. C. (2005). Birds on the wire: Troping teenage girlhood throughtelephony in mid-twentieth-century US media culture.*Cultural Studies, 19* (5), 568–601.

Kendall, L. (1996). MUDer? I hardly know HER! Adventures of a feminist MUDder," In L. Cherny & E. R. Weise (Eds.), *Wired women: Gender and new realities in cyberspace* (pp. 216–217). Seattle, WA: Seal.

Kornblum, J. (2005. October 31). Teens wear their hearts on their blog. *USA Today* (p. 1D). Retrieved July 7, 2006, from http://www.usatoday.com/tech/news/techinnovations/2005-10-30-teen-blogs_x.htm

Kornblum, J. (2006, January 9). Teens hang out at MySpace; Web is now a real place to socialize. *USA Today* (p. 1D). Retrieved July 7, 2006, from http://www.usatoday.com/tech/news/2006-01-08-myspace-teens_x.htm

Lamb, S. (2001). *The secret lives of girls: What good girls really do—sex play, aggression and their guilt*. New York: Free Press.

Lenhart, A. (2005). *Protecting teens online*. Washington, DC: Pew Internet & American Life Project. Retrieved July 1, 2006, from http://www.pewinternet.org/PPF/r/152/report_display.asp

Lenhart, A., & Madden, M. (2005). *Teen content creators and consumers*. Washington, DC: Pew Internet & American Life Project. Retrieved July 1, 2006, from http://www.pewinternet.org/PPF/r/166/report_display.asp.

Lenhart, A., Madden, M., & Hitlin, P. (2005). *Teens and technology: Youth are leading the transition to a fully wired and mobile nation*. Washington, DC: Pew Internet & American Life Project. Retrieved July 1, 2006 from http://www.pewinternet.org/report_display.asp?r=162.

Lenhart, A., Rainie, L., & Lewis, O. (2001, July). Teenage life online: The rise of the instant-message generation and the Internet's impact on friendships and family relationships, Pew Internet and the American Life Project. Retrieved March 29, 2004, from the World Wide Web: http://www.pewinternet.org/reports/toc.asp?Report=36

Leonardi, P. M. (2003). Problematizing "new media": Culturally based perceptions of cell phones, computers among United States' Latinos. *Critical Studies in Media Communication, 20*(2), 160–179.

Lesko, N. (2001). *Act your age! A cultural construction of adolescence.* New York: Routledge Falmer.

Lewis, C., & Fabos, B. (2000). But will it work in the heartland? A response and illustration. *Journal of Adolescent & Adult Literacy, 43*(5), 462–469.

Lewis, C., & Finders, M. (2002). Implied adolescents and implied teachers: A generation gap for new times. In D. E. Alvermann (Ed.), *New literacies and digital technologies: A focus on adolescent learners* (pp. 101–113). New York: Peter Lang.

Lindlof, T. (1995). *Qualitative communication research methods.* Thousand Oaks, CA: Sage.

Livingstone, S. (2002). *Young people and new media.* London: Sage.

Longhurst, D. (1989). *Gender, genre and narrative pleasure.* London: Unwin.

MacDonald, J. (2005, May 25). Teens: It's a diary. Adults: It's unsafe. *Christian Science Monitor, 97*(127), 11–13.

Martin, M. (1991*). "Hello Central?": Gender, technology, and culture in the formation of telephone systems.* Montreal; Kingston: McGill-Queen's University Press.

Martin, M. C., & Gentry, J. W. (1997). Stuck in the model trap: The effects of beautiful models in ads on female pre-adolescents and adolescents. *The Journal of Advertising, 26*(2), 19–33.

Mazzarella, S. R. (1999). The "Superbowl of all dates": Teenage girl magazines and the commodification of the perfect prom. In S. R. Mazzarella & N. Pecora (Eds.), *Growing up girls: Popular culture and the construction of identity* (pp. 97–112). New York: Peter Lang.

Mazzarella, S. R. (2005). Claiming a space: The cultural economy of teen girl fandom on the Web. In S. Mazzarella (Ed.), *Girl wide web: Girls, the Internet, and the negotiation of identity* (pp. 141–160). New York: Peter Lang.

Mazzarella, S. R., & Pecora, N. (1999). Introduction. In S. R. Mazzarella & N. Pecora (Eds.), *Growing up girls: Popular culture and the construction of identity* (pp. 1–14). New York: Peter Lang.

McLaren, P. (1993) Border disputes: Multicultural narrative, identity formation, and critical pedagogy in post modern America. In D. McLaughlin & W. Tierney (Eds.), *Naming silenced lives—personal narratives and the process of educational change* (pp. 201–235). New York: Routledge.

McRobbie, A. (1982). Jackie: An ideology of adolescent feminism. In B. Waites & T. Martin (Eds.), *Popular culture: Past and present* (pp. 263–283). London: Open University Press.

McRobbie, A. (1997). *Back to reality? Social experience and cultural studies*. Manchester: Manchester University Press.

Merskin, D. (2005). Making an about face: Jammer girls and the World Wide Web. In S. Mazzarella (Ed.), *Girl wide web: Girls, the Internet, and the negotiation of identity* (pp. 51–68). New York: Peter Lang.

Milkie, M. (1994, October). Social world approach to cultural studies: Mass media and gender in the adolescent peer group. *Journal of Contemporary Ethnography, 23*(3), 354–380.

Milkie, M. (1999). Social comparisons, reflected appraisals, media: The impact of pervasive beauty images on black and white girl self concepts. *Social Psychology Quarterly, 62*(2), 190–210.

Miller, H. (1995, June). *The presentation of self in electronic life: Goffman on the Internet*. Paper presented at Embodied Knowledge and Virtual Space conference, Goldsmiths' College, University of London. Retrieved March 9, 2004, from the World Wide Web: http://ess.ntu.ac.uk/miller/cyberpsych/goffman.htm

Munro, P. (1998). *Subject to fiction*. Buckingham, UK: Open University Press.

New Media Age. (March, 2006). One-third of all search engine users click through to etailers *New Media Age,* p. 13.

Orenstein, P. (1994). *Schoolgirls: Young, self-esteem, and the confidence gap*. New York: Doubleday.

Orr Vered, K. (1998). Blue group boys play Incredible Machine, girls play hopscotch: Social discourse and gendered play at the computer. In J. Sefton-Green (Ed.), *Digital diversions: Youth culture in the age of multimedia* (pp. 43–61). London: UCL Press.

Perseus Corporation. (2005). The blogging geyser: 31.6 million hosted blogs, growing to 53.4 million by year end. Retrieved March 1, 2006, from http://www.perseus.com/blogsurvey/geyser.html

Pipher, M. (1994). *Reviving Ophelia: Saving the selves of adolescent girls*. New York: Ballentine

Radway, J. (1984). *Reading the romance: Women, patriarchy and popular literature*. Chapel Hill: University of North Carolina Press.

Rakow, L. F. (1992). *Gender on the line: Women, the telephone, and community life*. Chicago: University of Illinois Press.

Reid, E. (1991). *Electropolis: Communication and community on Internet Relay Chat.* Unpublished honor's thesis. University of Melbourne, Australia. Retrieved March 9, 2004, from the World Wide Web: http://eserver.org/cyber/reid.txt

Rheingold, H. (1993). *The virtual community: Homesteading on the electronic frontier.* Reading, MA: Addison-Wesley.

Ribak, R. (2001). Like immigrants: Negotiating power in the face of the home computer, *New Media & Society, 3*(2) 220–238.

Rogers-Cherland, M. (1994). *Private practices: Girls reading fiction and constructing identity.* London: Taylor & Francis.

Ruddick, S. (1989). *Maternal thinking: Toward a politics of peace.* Boston: Beacon.

Scodari, C. (2005). You're sisteen, you're dutiful, you're online. "Fangirls" and the negotiation of age and/or gender subjectivities in TV newsgroups. In S. Mazzarella (Ed.), *Girl wide web: Girls, the Internet, and the negotiation of identity* (pp. 105–120). New York: Peter Lang.

Sefton-Green, J. (1998). Introduction: Being young in the digital age. In J. Sefton-Green (Ed.), *Digital diversions: Youth culture in the age of multimedia* (pp. 1–20). London: UCL Press.

Shostak, M. (1981). *Nisa: The life and words of a !Kung woman.* Cambridge, MA: Harvard University Press.

Simmons, R. (2002). *Odd girl out: The hidden culture of aggression in girls.* Orlando, FL: Harcourt.

Smith, S. (2004, April). Google vs. Yahoo!: Battling for the search marketing kingdom, *Media,* 5 (4), 24–28.

Stephenson, W. (1988). Play theory of mass communication broadly considered. In W. Stephenson (Ed.), *The play theory of mass communication* (pp. 190–206). New Brunswick, NJ: Transaction Books.

Stern, S. R. (1999, Winter). Adolescent girls' expression on Web home pages: Spirited, somber and self-conscious sites. *Convergence, 5*(4), 22–41.

Stern, S. R. (2001). Sexual selves on the World Wide Web: Adolescent girls' homepages as sites for sexual self-expression. In J. Brown, J. Steele, & K. Walsh-Childers (Eds.), *Sexual teens/sexual media: Investigating media's influence on adolescent sexuality* (pp. 265–286). Hillsdale, NJ: Lawrence Erlbaum.

Stern, S. R. (2004). Expressions of identity online: Prominent features and gender differences in adolescents' WWW home pages. *Journal of Broadcasting & Electronic Media, 48*(2), 218–243.

Swartz, D. (1997). *The sociology of Pierre Bourdieu.* Chicago: University of Chicago Press.

Talbot, M. (2002, February 24). Girls just want to be mean: Mean girls and the new movement to tame them. *The New York Times Magazine,* 24–29, 40, 58, 64–65.

Taylor, B., & Conrad, C. (1992). Narratives of sexual harassment: Organizational dimensions. *Journal of Applied Communication Research, 17,* 401–418.

Thiel, S. (2004). Shifting identities, creating new paradigms: Analyzing the narratives of women online journalists. *Feminist Media Studies, 4*(1), 21–36.

Thiel, S. (2005). "IM Me": Identity construction and gender negotiation in the world of girls and instant messaging. In S. Mazzarella (Ed.), *Girl wide web: Girls, the Internet, and the negotiation of identity* (pp. 51–68). New York: Peter Lang.

Tobin, J. (1998). An American Otaku (or, a boy's virtual life on the Net). In J. Sefton-Green (Ed.), *Digital diversions: Youth culture in the age of multimedia* (pp. 106–127). London: UCL.

Tronto, J. (1993). *Moral boundaries: A political argument for an ethic of care.* New York: Routledge.

Tufte, B. (2003). Girls in the new media landscape. *Nordicom Review, 24*(1), 71–78.

Turkle, S. (1995). *Life on the screen: Identity in the age of the Internet.* New York: Simon & Schuster.

Tyre, P. (2006, January 30). The trouble with boys. *Newsweek,* 44–55.

Visweswaran, K. (1994). *Fictions of feminist ethnography.* Minneapolis: University of Minnesota Press.

Walker, M. (2001, March). Engineering identities. *British Journal of Sociology of Education, 22*(75), 15–30.

Wallace, P. (1999). *The psychology of the Internet.* New York: Cambridge University Press.

Walsh, S.F. (2005). Gender, power, and social interaction: How Bluejean Online constructs adolescent girlhood. In S. Mazzarella (Ed.), *Girl wide web: Girls, the Internet, and the negotiation of identity* (pp. 69-84). New York: Peter Lang.

Ward, C. J. (2003). *African American girls, rap music, and the negotiation of identity: An analysis of gender, race, and class in relation to rap music videos*. Unpublished doctoral dissertation, University of Iowa, Iowa City.

Willinsky, J., & Hunniford, M. R. (1993). Reading the romance younger: The mirrors and fears of a preparatory literature. In L. Christian-Smith (Ed.), *Texts of desire: Essays on fiction, femininity and schooling* (pp. 87–105). London: Falmer.

Wolf, N. (1991). *The beauty myth: How images of beauty are used against women*. New York: William Murrow.

Woods, B. (2002). ActiveBuddy retires SmarterChild on AIM. *AtNewYork.com.* Retrieved July 1, 2006, from http://www.atnewyork.com/news/article.php/1381631

mediated youth

Sharon R. Mazzarella
General Editor

Vol. 2

Grounded in cultural studies, books in this series will study the cultures, artifacts, and media of children, tweens, teens, and college-aged youth. Whether studying television, popular music, fashion, sports, toys, the Internet, self-publishing, leisure, clubs, school, cultures/activities, film, dance, language, tie-in merchandising, concerts, subcultures, or other forms of popular culture, books in this series go beyond the dominant paradigm of traditional scholarship on the effects of media/culture on youth. Instead, authors endeavor to understand the complex relationship between youth and popular culture. Relevant studies would include, but are not limited to studies of how youth negotiate their way through the maze of corporately-produced mass culture; how they themselves have become cultural producers; how youth create "safe spaces" for themselves within the broader culture; the political economy of youth culture industries; the representational politics inherent in mediated coverage and portrayals of youth; and so on. Books that provide a forum for the "voices" of the young are particularly encouraged. The source of such voices can range from in-depth interviews and other ethnographic studies to textual analyses of cultural artifacts created by youth.

For further information about the series and submitting manuscripts, please contact:

SHARON R. MAZZARELLA
Communication Studies Department
Clemson University
Clemson, SC 29634

To order other books in this series, please contact our Customer Service Department at:

(800) 770-LANG (within the U.S.)
(212) 647-7706 (outside the U.S.)
(212) 647-7707 FAX

Or browse online by series at WWW.PETERLANG.COM